Berenson clearly knows how to connect with u...undergraduate students who will be
encountering data management techniques fo...
examples, these techniques will make it easier...
you track what you have done when you want...

—**John A. Johnson, PhD,** Professor Emeritus of Psy...chology, ...Pennsylvania State University...
University Park

When it comes to managing and documenting data, students need clear and detailed
guidance. In a crisp and engaging style, Berenson delivers—all student researchers
will benefit from this helpful book.

—**Glenn Geher, PhD,** Professor of Psychology, State University of New York, New Paltz

Berenson has produced a detailed yet approachable guide for creating reproducible
research projects. Her recommended workflows smartly integrate reproducible
practices into the research process, in recognition of the challenge of retrofitting
reproducibility into a project once completed. Undergraduate students as well as
seasoned professionals will benefit from this practical book.

—**Norm Medeiros, MLIS,** Associate Librarian, Haverford College, and Codirector,
Project TIER, Haverford, PA

This book contains principles and practices that are essential for conducting data-
driven research efficiently and transparently. Berenson has distilled these fundamental
concepts into a concise and accessible format, yet detailed enough to give students
the concrete guidance they need to adopt the recommended methods. Following
these guidelines will reduce the stress students sometimes experience when conducting empirical research, increase their productivity, and ultimately enhance the
scientific validity of their work. This will be a key resource for instructors wishing to
introduce students to the transparency movement that is reshaping the way research
is done in psychology and across the social sciences.

—**Richard Ball, PhD,** Professor of Economics, Haverford College, and Codirector, Project TIER,
Haverford, PA

The path out of the replication crisis is transparency in scientific practice. Berenson
provides us with three essential components of a well-tuned guide. First, the topic is
invaluable as psychology works to address the replication crisis. Second, the writing
is clear and focused. Third, the advice is practical. This book is highly recommended.

—**Scott Bates, PhD,** Associate Vice President and Associate Dean, Office of Research and
Graduate Studies, and Professor, Department of Psychology, Utah State University, Logan

Simply put, we're forgetful, and careful documentation now will save our future
selves and collaborators a lot of trouble, time, and inaccuracy. In this book, Berenson
provides a much-needed introduction and template for readers interested in incorpo-
rating such practices into their existing research workflows.

—**Jeffrey Spies, PhD,** Cofounder and Chief Technology Officer, Center for Open Science,
Charlottesville, VA

Managing Your Research Data and Documentation

Concise Guides to Conducting Behavioral, Health, and Social Science Research Series

Designing and Proposing Your Research Project
   Jennifer Brown Urban and Bradley Matheus van Eeden-Moorefield

Managing Your Research Data and Documentation
   Kathy R. Berenson

Writing Your Psychology Research Paper
   Scott A. Baldwin

Managing Your Research Data and Documentation

KATHY R. BERENSON

CONCISE GUIDES TO CONDUCTING BEHAVIORAL, HEALTH, AND SOCIAL SCIENCE RESEARCH

AMERICAN PSYCHOLOGICAL ASSOCIATION • *Washington, DC*

The opinions and statements published are the responsibility of the authors, and such opinions and statements do not necessarily represent the policies of the American Psychological Association.

All trademarks depicted within this book, including trademarks appearing as a part of a screenshot, figure, or other image are included solely for the purpose of illustration and are the property of their respective holders. The use of the trademarks in no way indicates any relationship with, or endorsement by, the holders of said trademarks. SPSS is a registered trademark of International Business Machines Corporation.

Published by
American Psychological Association
750 First Street, NE
Washington, DC 20002
www.apa.org

APA Order Department
P.O. Box 92984
Washington, DC 20090-2984
Phone: (800) 374-2721; Direct: (202) 336-5510
Fax: (202) 336-5502; TDD/TTY: (202) 336-6123
Online: http://www.apa.org/pubs/books
E-mail: order@apa.org

In the U.K., Europe, Africa, and the Middle East, copies may be ordered from
Eurospan Group
c/o Pegasus Drive
Stratton Business Park
Biggleswade Bedfordshire
SG18 8TQ United Kingdom
Phone: +44 (0) 1767 604972
Fax: +44 (0) 1767 601640
Online: https://www.eurospanbookstore.com/apa
E-mail: eurospan@turpin-distribution.com

Typeset in Minion by Circle Graphics, Inc., Columbia, MD

Printer: Edwards Brothers Malloy, Lillington, NC
Cover Designer: Naylor Design, Washington, DC

Library of Congress Cataloging-in-Publication Data
Names: Berenson, Kathy R., author.
Title: Managing your research data and documentation / Kathy R. Berenson.
Description: Washington, DC : American Psychological Association, [2018] |
    Series: Concise guides to conducting behavioral, health, and social
    science research series | Includes bibliographical references and index.
Identifiers: LCCN 2017033361 | ISBN 9781433827099 | ISBN 1433827093
Subjects: LCSH: Psychology—Research. | Psychology—Methodology.
Classification: LCC BF76.5 .B47 2018 | DDC 150.72—dc23
LC record available at https://lccn.loc.gov/2017033361

British Library Cataloguing-in-Publication Data
A CIP record is available from the British Library.

Printed in the United States of America
First Edition

http://dx.doi.org/10.1037/0000068-000

10 9 8 7 6 5 4 3 2 1

For Devin

Contents

Series Foreword

Why are you reading this book? Perhaps you have recently been assigned to write a research paper in an undergraduate course. Maybe you are considering graduate school in one of the behavioral, health, or social science disciplines, such as psychology, public health, nursing, or medicine, and know that having a strong research background gives you a major advantage in getting accepted. Maybe you simply want to know how to conduct research in these areas. Or perhaps you are interested in actually conducting your own study. Regardless of the reason, you are probably wondering—how do I start?

Conducting research can be analogous to cooking a meal for several people. Doing so involves planning (e.g., developing a menu), having adequate resources (e.g., having the correct pots, pans, carving knives, plates), knowing what the correct ingredients are (e.g., what spices are needed), properly cooking the meal (e.g., grilling vs. baking, knowing how long it takes to cook), adequately presenting the food (e.g., making the meal look appetizing), and so forth. Conducting research also involves planning, proper execution, having adequate resources, and presenting one's project in a meaningful manner. Both activities also involve creativity, persistence, caring, and ethical behavior. But just like cooking a meal for several people, conducting research should follow one of my favorite pieces of advice—"remember that the devil is in the details." If you want your dinner guests to find your meal tasty, you need to follow a recipe properly and measure the ingredients accurately (e.g., too much or little of some of the ingredients can make the entrée taste awful). Similarly, conducting research without properly paying attention to details can lead to erroneous results.

Okay, but what about your question—"How do I start?" This American Psychological Association book series provides detailed but user-friendly guides for conducting research in the behavioral, health, and social sciences from start to finish. I cannot help but think of another food analogy here— that is, the series will focus on everything from "soup to nuts." These short, practical books will guide the student/researcher through each stage of the process of developing, conducting, writing, and presenting a research project. Each book will focus on a single aspect of research, for example, choosing a research topic, following ethical guidelines when conducting research with humans, using appropriate statistical tools to analyze your data, and deciding which measures to use in your project. Each volume in this series will help you attend to the details of a specific activity. All volumes will help you complete important tasks and will include illustrative examples. Although the theory and conceptualization behind each activity are important to know, these books will focus especially on the "how to" of conducting research, so that you, the research student, can successfully carry out a meaningful research project.

This particular volume, by Kathy Berenson, focuses on managing the data that you will eventually collect as part of your study, as well as analyzing the results in such a manner as to allow you to make reasonable and valid conclusions. Especially helpful is the inclusion of illustrative examples using SPSS statistical software. Emphasized throughout the volume is the need to be organized—more importantly, Dr. Berenson demonstrates how to do so. She also underscores the need to *document* everything you do from beginning to end. Conducting a study can be a daunting task— using this book can make it easier.

So, the answer to the question "How do I start?" is simple: Just turn the page and begin reading!

Best of luck!

—Arthur M. Nezu, PhD, DHL, ABPP
Series Editor

Preface

Concerns about the transparency and replicability of research in the behavioral sciences have recently put a spotlight on the need to take documentation of data management and analysis more seriously. But documentation procedures are almost never formally taught, and technological advances have made many once-standard record-keeping practices obsolete. Many young researchers, familiar only with today's menu-driven, point-and-click statistics packages, have no system at all for documenting or saving their work. These trends are a problem not just for research replicability but also for learning. Analyzing and modifying data files without saving the executed commands keeps these processes mysterious and rushed and prevents many students from being able to really see, check, and understand the analyses they do. Wishing to assign my students an introductory how-to manual on data management and documentation that would guide them through the process of creating replication documentation for their psychology major capstone projects, I soon realized I would have to write it myself.

I am grateful for the helpful feedback I received in the process of writing this book from editor Beth Hatch and three anonymous reviewers. I am also grateful to William R. Shadish for his encouragement. I regret that he passed away before I had an opportunity to meet him or work with him on the manuscript that he inspired me to write. Thanks to John Bernstein for turning my fuzzy ideas for figures into high-resolution reality. Thanks to the many Gettysburg College students who tried out portions of the manuscript while working in my research lab or completing capstone projects during 2015–2017, especially Tess M. Anderson, Jillian V. Glazer, and Melissa P. Menna. Students' honest reactions to the material were crucial in shaping the direction of the book, which is, after all, meant for them. Finally, thanks to Devin McKinney, for everything and more, with all my love.

Managing Your Research Data and Documentation

Introduction

If you needed a surgeon to operate on your brain, you would want to entrust your care to someone with training and expertise, perhaps even brilliance, in brain surgery. But brain surgery isn't the only thing you'd expect this person to do well and take seriously. Preoperative and postoperative procedures are important, even if they are not brain surgery per se. Indeed, if while lying on the operating table you were to hear your doctor say, "Never mind the handwashing: I'm a brain surgeon, not a cleaner," you would be smart to grab your paper hospital gown and make a run for the exit.

In the research world, data management and documentation can be seen as similar to essential pre- and postoperative tasks. They aren't data analysis per se; they are the crucial things that have to be done before and after data analysis. Students, professors, and other researchers all find themselves tempted to skip these procedures so they can focus their time

http://dx.doi.org/10.1037/0000068-001
Managing Your Research Data and Documentation, by K. R. Berenson

and attention on theories, predictions, and results. When you feel this way, remind yourself that you don't want to be like a brain surgeon who operates with dirty hands. Though data management and documentation may not be as intellectually stimulating or prestigious as other parts of the research process, even the greatest results will be worthless unless these basic steps are also done well.

THE IMPORTANCE OF DOCUMENTING EVERYTHING YOU DO WITH YOUR DATA

Replicability is a central value in science. It is part of the overall idea that a meaningful result did not just happen randomly but can be counted on to happen repeatedly. If a study you conducted is replicable (or reproducible), someone else who conducts your study over again from scratch, copying exactly what you did, will get the same results (Open Science Collaboration, 2015). Psychology is one of several scientific fields in which low rates of replicability have received a lot of criticism from researchers and the popular media. Indeed, many well-known and cherished ideas in psychology are now being called into question because the famous studies that supported them have not been able to be reproduced. In a recent major attempt to replicate 100 published psychology studies, only 36% obtained the same results (Open Science Collaboration, 2015). One reason many attempts to replicate psychology research studies fail is that it is often difficult to match closely enough what the original researchers did. For example, it might matter whether participants complete the study on a computer rather than on paper or have a different cultural background from the participants in the original study (Gilbert, King, Pettigrew, & Wilson, 2016). Trying to replicate previous studies and make future studies more readily replicable is an important goal in psychology research today. It is also an incredibly daunting one because it is so complex and so broad.

When faced with a daunting goal, it's often helpful to break the goal down into specific parts that are more manageable. Before worrying about being able to replicate entire studies, researchers should perhaps first solve the problem of being able to replicate what one another does with their data. For example, if your friends conducted a study and gave you all their original data to analyze yourself, would you be able to find the same results your friends did? Don't count on it. The procedures that are broadly called *data management* (preparing your data to be analyzed by checking and fixing problems and computing variables) and *data analysis* (obtaining descriptive and inferential statistics) involve making many decisions, and these decisions can have a large influence on the results you ultimately find (Simmons, Nelson, & Simonsohn, 2011). Unless you knew exactly everything your friends decided to do with their data from the beginning, you might not be able to retrace their steps or even know where to start. Although documentation of data management and analysis is not all there is to the replicability of research, this small part is a crucial one.

You have probably been taught that it is necessary to have the correct documentation to back up everything you say in psychology research papers—specifically, citations and references in the format required by the American Psychological Association (APA). When you're doing original research—conducting your own analyses and maybe even collecting your own data—the documentation relating to your data management and analyses is just as important. In fact, it is an ethical responsibility of psychologists to share necessary data and documentation with other researchers who wish to verify their results, as described in Ethical Standards 6.01, Documentation of Professional and Scientific Work and Maintenance of Records, and 8.14, Sharing Research Data for Verification, of the American Psychological Association's (APA's) *Ethical Principles of Psychologists and Code of Conduct* (APA, 2017; see http://www.apa.org/ethics/code/index.aspx) and in the sixth edition of the *Publication Manual of the American Psychological Association*, section 1.08 (APA, 2010).

Enabling outsiders to examine our work helps inform and improve future studies and therefore has possible repercussions for the lives of many people. Let's say you do a study and publish the results. When other researchers and students read your paper and develop projects that build on it, understanding exactly what you did may turn out to be important for their careers. Moreover, the results of many scientific studies can have important effects on the public at large. The population being investigated by your research could be hurt by a false positive or false negative result and would benefit from the ability of other researchers to clear up the scientific record.

Requiring you to properly document how you handled your data is not just about your project grade; it isn't even really about you or your reputation. Developing these skills promotes the progress of science and the greater good.

A renewed emphasis on teaching research documentation practices is necessary at this point because recent technological advances have made research documentation both more convenient and more complicated. Decades ago, everything researchers did was on paper, and documenting research largely meant storing a lot of file boxes and folders. Clunky old computers also required a built-in system of documentation; the only way they could analyze your data was if you typed up a set of commands, which would then be kept for future use and as a record of what was done. But what are the comparable procedures for documenting research today? Being able to access data anywhere means that files can easily end up scattered and lost. People are also often tempted to do things to their data with a point and click or by directly typing into their data file—conveniences that are quite dangerous to the integrity of scientific research. Today, new procedures for documenting data management and analysis are necessary to achieve the level of record keeping that at less convenient times we had by default.

The culture of academic psychology has historically focused solely on the final products of research, so that careful behind-the-scenes documentation often went unrewarded and untaught. The chances are that many of your professors and mentors were left to figure out documentation procedures on their own. But now that culture is changing because of renewed attention to the replicability of science and rapid advances in technology. Gone are the days when papers covered with illegible scribbles were considered sufficient documentation for a research project. Doing research today requires knowing how to keep records of our work that others—supervisors, collaborators, reviewers, editors, and other researchers—can readily understand and use. As research documentation moves from musty storage facilities to downloadable files, it is time to take this process out of the dark and actually teach it. This is something we all do and that we all have to do. It should not have to be treated like a dirty little secret.

To ensure that research documentation does get done effectively and systematically, students and beginning researchers have to be taught to do it and how, step by step. Along these lines, Richard Ball and Norm Medeiros at Haverford College developed Project TIER (Teaching Integrity in Empirical Research) to help prepare faculty to better teach data management and documentation procedures to undergraduate students conducting original research projects in the social sciences. The suggestions offered in this book were informed and inspired by the TIER documentation protocol (which can be downloaded from their website at http://www.projecttier.org) and are compatible with it—but adapted to suit better the specific needs of psychological science specifically.[1]

GOAL AND PRINCIPLES BEHIND THIS BOOK

This book provides guidelines and step-by-step instructions for managing data and documentation in psychological research. It is designed to meet the needs of undergraduate or graduate level psychology students learning to conduct research, whether for a capstone or thesis, independent study, laboratory course, or research assistant position in a psychology lab. Though this book gives examples in the Statistical Package for the Social Sciences (SPSS®),[2] the procedures it describes can be carried out with any programmable statistical package, such as SAS, R, or Stata.[3] The procedures the book recommends are designed to help people conduct research in ways that are compatible with sound and

---

[1]Compared with the TIER protocol, this book places less emphasis on the creation of metadata and importable files because students learning to do psychology research typically collect their own data in SPSS or in formats that SPSS can easily read. (Students who are not collecting their own data or who require data importation commands will find these topics covered in appendices.) However, this book places greater emphasis on documentation of variable computations (e.g., making a scale from several individual items) because this is a common aspect of working with data in psychology. Missing data and cases requiring exclusion are also addressed because they are such common issues when using data collected from living research subjects. Finally, this book makes substantial modifications to the TIER documentation protocol to encourage consideration of the participant confidentiality requirements important in many types of psychological research.

[2]SPSS is a registered trademark of International Business Machines Corporation.

[3]Excel may be used for data entry, but it is not recommended for data management and analysis because it cannot be programmed with the executable command files that are essential for carrying out these procedures in a fully replicable and documented way. Excel is similarly considered incompatible with the Project TIER protocol (Owens, 2014).

ethical research practices for improving scientific replicability. Because these procedures help researchers stay more organized and keep better records, practicing them can also help people feel less overwhelmed and gain a greater sense of mastery when working with data, in turn allowing people to think more deeply and creatively about their data and get more out of the experience.[4]

The goal of the procedures described in this book is to have a researcher who reads your paper be readily able to recreate your final results, starting from the beginning with the same data file(s) with which you originally started. To make this goal possible, this book is designed on the following principles, which correspond to the four central components of the *project folder* that you will create to store what is needed for your project and that also correspond to the four upcoming chapters. Each principle is the focus of a subsequent chapter in this book.

- Keep well-organized copies of all project files, such as institutional review board (IRB) approvals, materials, logs, and participant information (Chapter 2).
- Keep read-only copies of your data file(s) in the original, untouched state they were in before you started modifying them in any way (Chapter 3).
- Create reader-friendly command files to document everything you do with your data (instead of saving endless pages of output and instead of typing up a separate set of descriptive documents; Chapter 4).
- Create a concise folder of replication documentation to correspond to the final version of your paper, suitable for use by outside researchers (Chapter 5).

The remainder of this book explains one folder at a time each of these components of your project folder and what makes them useful and important. Before we proceed, though, let's start with an overview of your project folder and its structure.

---

[4]Being able to manage data is also a skill of practical value to develop because it is associated with more job prospects and higher salary even for students who do not pursue a career in science (Blumenstyk, 2016).

YOUR PROJECT FOLDER

When you are starting your project, one of your first steps will be to create a series of computer folders (on a specific computer or in cloud storage) to contain and organize all your work while you are completing your project. If your paper is published, you will keep the project folder that is associated with it for at least 5 more years, as required by the APA (APA Ethical Standard 6.01, Documentation of Professional and Scientific Work and Maintenance of Records), in case researchers require additional information.

You will begin by creating a folder for your project and give it an informative, clearly identifying name (rather than a generic or vague one such as "Project folder" or "Psych project" or even "Developmental psych final project"). If you're handing this folder in for a class, keep in mind that professors are often frustrated when they receive many identical-looking assignments that cannot be easily matched to their creators (e.g., dozens of electronic documents that are all called "final paper"). A better name for your folder might include the last names of the individual(s) doing the project and/or an abbreviated project title, along with the course number and year (e.g., "Bond Psych 399 Spring 2017" or "Perfectionism and Rumination Psych 399 Fall 2016"). Research labs similarly use abbreviations, nicknames, or numbering systems to identify particular projects and distinguish them from one another (e.g., "Attributions Study 2"). What is important is that the project folder's name uniquely refers to the specific project in a way that is recognizable and sensible to everyone involved.

Next, create the subfolders needed within your project folder, as shown in Figure 1.1. The order in which you're creating these folders or files is similar to the order in which you'll fill them and use them. You'll first create files for private use by you and other members of your research team in carrying out and writing up your study. Afterward, you will prepare replication documentation for sharing and/or storing in a public archive. Notice that the subfolders in Figure 1.1 are numbered (e.g., 1, 1a, 1b, etc.) so that they will stay in this same fixed order on your computer.

The following is an overview of the various subfolders and the steps you will take to fill them as you complete your project from beginning to

📁 [Name of your project folder]

    📁 1. Working files

        📁 1a. Working data files (temporary)

        📁 1b. Output files (temporary/optional)

        📁 1c. Paper drafts (temporary/optional)

    📁 2. Project files

        📁 2a. Official records

        📁 2b. Materials

        📁 2c. Logs

        📁 2d. Participant information (may have passwords)

    📁 3. Data files

        📁 3a. Original data and/or source data and metadata

            (subfolders may have deletion dates and passwords)

        📁 3b. Data for processing

        📁 3c. Analysis data (optional)

    📁 4. Command files

    📁 5. Replication documentation for [project folder name or project or paper name]

        📁 5a. Read me, paper, and related documents

            📄 Read me

            📄 [Paper name]

            📄 Approved project plan or proposal or preregistration (if applicable)

        📁 5b. Replication data for processing

        📁 5c. Replication command files: SPSS and PDF versions

        📁 5d. Replication analysis data, data appendix, optional PDFs of final output

        📁 5e. Replication source data and metadata (if applicable)

Figure 1.1

Project folder.

end. Many of these subfolders will stay empty for a while, but that's OK. You'll be learning how to fill up the subfolders within your project folder throughout the rest of this book, and you might want to refer back to this overview as you read further ahead.

Working Files

Your *Working Files* folder is a place to temporarily store the files you are actively working with while your project is in progress. The folder contains three major subfolders. The *Working Data* folder will be kept empty most of the time and serves only one purpose: to remind you never to modify directly any of the data files that you keep archived in your Data Files folder (described later). That is, when you are doing data management or analyses, you will always start by putting a copy of the data file that you want to work with into your Working Data folder and run the applicable command file(s) on that temporary copy. When you're finished working with it, you can choose to save that working data file as an optional Analysis Data file (described later) or to delete it. In addition, you may want to optionally store *Output Files* and *Paper Drafts* in progress in your Working Files folder. These files can be considered "working files" in that they are meant to be temporary and do not have to be saved, but it can be helpful to keep them readily accessible for looking up information while you're working on your paper. (See Chapter 2 for a suggestion on how to keep multiple drafts of the same document organized by labeling them with the date they were created.)

Project files, as described in Chapter 2, include various important documents that are not data or command files but that have to be preserved as records of your project. You will be able to start filling several of the Project Files subfolders with forms even before you collect any data. Your *Official Records* subfolder will contain your IRB submission and whatever other proposals or plans you submitted for approval prior to starting your study. Your *Materials* subfolder will store copies of things such as questionnaire packets, experiment instructions, and stimuli. Your *Logs* subfolder will contain a data issues log to keep track of potential problems with particular observations or cases. You will add to this log while collecting data and perhaps while managing or analyzing it. Depending on the needs of your project, you may benefit from keeping additional logs—for instance a data collection log, data entry log, or data analysis log. Finally, you will use the *Participant Information* subfolder to store any potentially identifying records (such as lists of names, contact information, or ID numbers) in password-protected files.

Data Files

You will keep all your data organized in your *Data Files* folder (see Chapter 3). When your data have been collected and/or entered, you will store your untouched data files in your *Original Data* folder. If you obtain your data from another source (rather than collect it yourself), you will store untouched copies of the source data along with metadata, as described in Appendix A. Your *Data for Processing* folder will contain your data files in SPSS format. If your original data files were in SPSS format to begin with, these will simply be duplicate copies. After all data management tasks have been completed, you can choose to save a copy of your data set(s) in ready-to-analyze form in an optional *Analysis Data* folder. In addition to a detailed discussion of each of these subfolders, Chapter 3 provides guidelines useful in creating data files, such as information about entering data and choosing names for your variables. The accompanying appendices address special topics related to data files, including metadata for data sets obtained from other sources (Appendix A), "tall" data files (with repeated observations of each variable; Appendix B), and instructions for ensuring accurate data entry (Appendix C).

Command Files

As described in Chapter 4, to manage and analyze your data, you will create command files for everything you do to manage and analyze your data. After an orientation to *command files* for people who may never have used (or even heard of) them before, Chapter 4 provides step-by-step instructions for many common data management tasks, including renaming variables, assigning variable labels and value labels, checking frequency tables for data errors, using missing data codes, handling missing data, excluding cases, computing variables (including reversing items and creating groups, z-scores, and scales), analyzing scale reliability, and working with subsets of your sample. Additional instructions for specialized data management tasks are covered in the appendices, including labeling and renaming many variables efficiently (Appendix D), importing data files (Appendix E), merging data files (Appendix F), and estimating missing values (Appendix G).

Replication Documentation

After you finish your analyses and write your paper, you'll put your paper and all the materials necessary for replication of your results into a publicly shareable *Replication Documentation* folder (see Chapter 5). The *Read Me* document will list or describe the files in your Replication Documentation folder and provide instructions for recreating the results reported in your paper. You'll check that the steps listed actually work by reproducing your own results yourself. You'll also include the final version of your paper and any documentation of the plans you made for your study prior to conducting it, such as a formal preregistration or an approved proposal. The Data for Processing files that you'll put in your shareable Replication Documentation folder will often be identical copies of the data files you've saved for private use. However, to be consistent with participant confidentiality and copyright laws, you may have to omit some information from the data files you share. You will create *replication command file(s)* by copying and editing the relevant portions of the command files you used to manage and analyze your data. Replication commands for data analysis will appear in the order in which they appear in your paper and have comments indicating the page on which the relevant results appear. Your replication command files will be saved as PDFs (as well as the standard SPSS command file format) to make it easier for readers to access them. You will save shareable Analysis Data file(s) containing the data used for the analyses reported in your paper (with the data already cleaned and variables computed). You will also create a *data appendix* document to provide variable information and descriptive statistics for every variable in the Analysis Data file. You can optionally create a PDF version of the final output of the analyses in your paper to store in this folder. Finally, if you obtained your data from another source and have permission to share it, you'll include a copy of your *Source Data* folder (and its Metadata subfolder) in your Replication Documentation folder. Submit your Replication Documentation folder along with your paper if requested by the professor, institution, or publication to which you are submitting it.

CONCLUDING COMMENTS

Some medical professionals might like to play loud, energizing music when they are getting ready to perform surgery, whereas others might prefer meditative silence, but these differences in style do not matter as long as all the essential cleaning and preparation gets done. Likewise, individual researchers may have their own tips and tricks for managing data and documentation or use different terms for their files and folders than the ones suggested here, but these differences in style don't matter either. What matters is that all researchers manage their data and documentation in ways that meet the increasingly strict standards that funding agencies, journals, and the field of scientific psychology at large are adopting to promote greater transparency and replicability of psychological research. This book will teach you a way to do this, step by step. And as you've just read, the first step is to create a well-organized set of empty subfolders for storing all the things you will be keeping in your project folder.

Before moving on, take a moment to consider that you're now the owner of the project folder you've just created. (Congratulations!) You will fill your folder with what it needs, update it, and keep it organized. You will ensure that your folder is regularly backed up, as a precaution against computer loss and other unthinkables. When you meet with your collaborators and/or professor to work on your project, you will have the materials you need from this folder ready (i.e., not assume that others will provide them or make others wait while you try to find them). You will put in the time it takes to become familiar with what is inside your folder and take responsibility for asking questions about things that are unclear to you. Owning this folder is a central part of making your research project truly yours.

2

Your Project Files

You will use your *Project Files* folder to store essential information relevant to your project in an organized, readily accessible manner. This folder contains four subfolders: Materials, Official Records, Logs, and Participant Information.

MATERIALS FOLDER

Because developing the materials for your project is a necessary early step in designing it, the *Materials* folder (see Figure 2.1) will typically be the first folder you can start to fill. Important materials to save include copies of forms, questionnaires, stimuli, study protocols (instructions or scripts), ads and letters used for participant recruitment, and so forth. Do not keep any data or participant information in your materials folder, only the blank materials, so that these materials can be readily viewed and shared without risk of compromising confidentiality.

http://dx.doi.org/10.1037/0000068-002
Managing Your Research Data and Documentation, by K. R. Berenson

📁 2b. Materials

📄 Questionnaire1.pdf

📄 Questionnaire2.pdf

📄 Debriefing Form.pdf

📄 Consent Form.pdf

📄 Student Newspaper Ad.pdf

📄 Experimenter Script.pdf

📁 Experiment Screenshots

📄 Screen1

📄 Screen2

📄 Screen3

📄 Screen4

(etc.)

📁 Experiment Programming Files

📁 Materials—Word versions

📁 Materials—old versions

Figure 2.1

Project materials.

If your research project involves a lot of materials, you should create subfolders to keep them organized. For example, if your study administers many sets of questionnaires, you can create a subfolder for them called "Questionnaires." Save all your materials as PDF documents to permanently preserve their formatting. To facilitate future reuse and editing, you might also save copies of your materials as Word or text files (in addition to the PDFs) in a subfolder with an appropriate label.

Today, many studies are conducted largely by computer, rather than through the use of printed forms. But because computer programs and websites have limited access and quickly become obsolete, it is important to create and save printable versions of these virtual research materials. If your study is conducted online, you should create a printable copy of it by converting it to a PDF or by taking screenshots. If your study is conducted using a computer program, you should save a copy of the file(s) used to run it, while also making sure to save it as a printable document. The printable version of your computer-based project is a valuable permanent record: It will remain accessible on almost any computer long after the Internet link to your study page has gone dead, or the particular program that ran your study has been replaced.

Long-term projects are likely to have multiple drafts of documents, and sometimes there are reasons to save the various drafts in addition to the most current one. To keep an organized record of multiple drafts of a document, create an "old versions" subfolder, and add the date to the end of the name of each file stored inside it. If the basic file name is kept consistent, and the added dates are written in YYMMDD format, the computer will automatically store them in their proper sequence. For example, you might have files called "student newspaper ad 150204," "student newspaper ad 150901," and "student newspaper ad 160421." If you are saving numerous old versions of things, you can use subfolders to organize them.

OFFICIAL RECORDS FOLDER

Your *Official Records* folder should contain evidence that your study has been approved by all applicable parties. For example, a copy of your approved institutional review board submission should be kept here. If your work involves any funding agencies, keep any documents they require (e.g., funded grant proposals, approved data management plans) here as well.

There is a growing movement to require researchers before they start their project to register everything they are going to measure and analyze to reduce biased reporting of research results and the tendency to publish false-positive results that cannot be replicated (Nosek et al., 2015). Consistent with this idea, you may be required by a professor, department, journal, or funding source to submit information ahead of time about all your proposed measures, analyses, and predictions. Requirements such as these are designed to make researchers more accountable and therefore help increase replicability of the research process. Because you may be asked to prove what you did (and didn't) predict in advance, you should keep copies of any study proposals, plans, or preregistration documents you submitted in your Official Records folder.

LOGS FOLDER

Your *Logs* folder will contain lists of information kept as SPSS data files, Excel spreadsheets, or Word documents (your preference). How many logs you keep will depend on the specific needs of your project. As described next, every project has to have a data issues log; many projects would also benefit from having a data analysis log to help you remember what analyses you've done and where to find the relevant command files. Logs are also recommended if you have to keep track of other procedures in progress. For example, a data collection log can be useful for assigning subjects to particular conditions and keeping track of how many have been run. A project that requires data entry might use a data entry log to record which cases have been entered. A project involving audio recordings of interviews might log which interviews have been transcribed. A project requiring researchers to make ratings of interview responses might log which cases have been rated. If you are ever in doubt about whether to keep a log, just do it; it's always better to have a log recording things you do not need than to be missing information that turns out to be crucial.

Projects of every size should have a data issues log. If you're lucky enough to have no data issues, you can show your log while you brag about it. But more often than not, data from living subjects will have issues. The data issues log will help you keep track of issues that arise while collecting and managing or analyzing your data, so you can decide whether particular cases or observations ought to be excluded from your results. To keep this log as complete and accurate as possible, add each potential issue to the log as soon as it happens or comes to your attention.

The following is an illustration of the kind of data issue that should be recorded. Perhaps you are running an experiment that examines the effects of meditation on mood. Half your participants are randomly assigned to do a 5-minute meditation exercise, whereas the other half spends 5 minutes doing some irrelevant task. One day, after your participant has finished meditating, but before you have a chance to assess their mood, the fire alarm goes off, forcing you and your participant to evacuate the lab. After several minutes, campus security tells you it is safe to return to the lab. Though you finish the study session by administering the mood questionnaires, it is likely that the fire alarm and evacuation will have influenced the participant's mood. Hence, it is important to have a record of what happened, as both a reminder and a justification for excluding this participant from your analyses.

Many different kinds of data issues may arise during data collection; other data issues may become apparent only when you are working with your data—for example, while entering data from paper questionnaires, you notice that a participant gave the same answer ("4") to an entire 200-item questionnaire packet, suggesting that they probably were not giving meaningful answers. Likewise, while doing analyses of a personality inventory that includes standardized validity scales, you may find that some participants scored off the charts in terms of the inconsistency of their responses or their efforts to present themselves in an implausibly positive or negative light. Issues such as these are important to record in your log as soon as you become aware of them, and it is better to document them late than not to document them at all.

Figure 2.2 depicts a data issues log for a large project, which for illustrative purposes involves many types of data (and perhaps an unusual amount of bad luck). Notice that these entries never include any identifying information (names, demographics) about the participants. It is to be hoped that in collecting your own data, you won't encounter so many strange issues. But just about anything can happen, and you should keep a record of it when it does.

PARTICIPANT INFORMATION

To protect participants' confidentiality, never attach or include their names with any of their data files. Likewise, materials containing participants' names (e.g., signed consent forms) should never contain the ID numbers

ID	Issue (followed by experimenter's initials)
#109	Questionnaire packet missing every other page due to a photocopier error. KRB
#166	Voice recorder didn't work. DM
#182	Experimenter ruined deception by laughing. Debriefed and ended study early. KRB
#234	Participant was texting while supposed to be measuring reaction time. DM
#258	Participant smelled like alcohol and seemed to slur their words. KRB
#293	Participant had a sneezing fit when measuring their reaction time. KRB
#306	Grand piano fell through the ceiling into the lab right after manipulation. DM
#325	Participant kept pressing wrong buttons, didn't seem to understand instructions. KRB
#328	Participant fell asleep when I turned the lights off to show them the video. DM

Figure 2.2

Data issues log.

linked with their data. Any potentially identifying participant information should be stored separately from the data in password-protected files in the *Participant Information* folder. The files in this folder may be SPSS data files, Excel spreadsheets, or Word documents—however you prefer to store the information. The specific files to be included will depend on your project; likewise, the nature of your project will guide decisions about how many different passwords you need. Individual Excel spreadsheets and Word documents are easily encrypted with password protection (go to "Permissions" on the File menu). Documents of all kinds can also be password protected if they are stored in locked folders.

Participant information files that include names or other specific identifying information often have an expiration date, after which they ought to be deleted. Unless you are doing a longitudinal study with plans to contact your participants for future follow-up, it is common to commit to deleting participant information when it is no longer needed (usually when data collection is finished or within a reasonable period afterward). A specific expiration date for this information is often specified on the project consent forms. If your study includes participant information that expires, you should put the expiration date in the title of the relevant files, so that instructions are clear to everyone who has the files or may someday inherit them. For example, you might call a file "Participant names— delete January 1, 2020."

One participant information file to keep might be an ongoing list, in alphabetical order, of all the names of the people who participated in your study. The purpose of a list like this would be to ensure that these people receive the credit or payment they deserve for participating and that no person participates twice. Leaving ID numbers and dates off this list allows members of the research team to use it without being able to match data with names, thereby maintaining the participants' privacy. Keeping the list in alphabetical order (rather than in order of study completion) is important for the same reason.

A participant contact information file (an alphabetized list of the participants' names and contact information) will be useful if you expect to have ongoing contact with your participants (e.g., for longitudinal studies). Again, keeping this file free of ID numbers will enable the research team to have access to the contact information for purposes of participant recruitment, scheduling, and so forth, without knowing which data belong to that individual.

The most private file to keep would be a participant ID file linking names with ID numbers. For example, you may have a file that contains the participant's ID number, name, and the date(s) of their participation in the study. The reason this file is so sensitive is that, unlike the previously mentioned files, this one can be used to connect specific responses to specific individuals. It often makes sense for this file to have a unique password, making it only accessible to specific members of the research team on a need-to-know basis.

If your project has any electronic copies of consent forms containing participants' names, they can also be kept in the participant information folder, where they will be locked with a password and separated from any of the data files.

You should record and keep only as much participant information as you need for your project. Often, a list of alphabetized participant names will be sufficient. But many short-term projects with no need to recontact the participants and no need to keep track of exactly which people participated can best protect participant privacy by not recording their names at all.

CONCLUDING COMMENTS

This chapter has focused on the various documents related to your project that you should save as part of your project records. The emphasis is on keeping these project documents clearly labeled and well organized and on handling any information that includes participants' names especially carefully.

Your Data Files

In this chapter, I discuss the data files you will be keeping as permanent records for your project: Original Data (and/or Source Data and Metadata), Data for Processing, and optionally, Analysis Data. When thinking about the files in these subfolders, remember that the point is to create them and keep them as "read-only" files in a completely untouched and unused state; therefore, any data management or data analysis you do will always use working data files in your Working Files folder, never these. In this chapter, I also cover some general guidelines for creating data files that may be helpful when it comes time to collect data, enter data, and/or name the variables in your data sets.

Note that although this chapter assumes that you will be analyzing your data in SPSS, the general ideas presented could be applied to any statistical package.

http://dx.doi.org/10.1037/0000068-003
Managing Your Research Data and Documentation, by K. R. Berenson

SUBFOLDERS IN YOUR DATA FOLDER

Original Data Folder

The *Original Data* folder that you keep for private use will contain a complete record of all the data you've collected, in whatever form you originally received it. In the simplest situation, the Original Data folder may contain just a single SPSS data file, but for more complex projects, it may include many data files of various kinds. For example, a longitudinal study may have three data files—a separate one for each time the participants filled out questionnaires in September, January, and May. Likewise, if you're doing a project that includes questionnaires, genetic tests, several laboratory experiments, and images from brain scans, you'll probably store each type of data in its own file. Some projects include so many data files that they should be organized using subfolders. All original data files should be set to be "read only" so they cannot be modified by accident. Some original data files, such as pictures, audio or video recordings of participants, or interview transcripts of participants in their own words, will also have to be kept locked or encrypted because their contents could potentially reveal participants' identities.

Although the typical data file is a spreadsheet with one row for each case (participant or subject), data files can also take other forms. Computerized multiple-trial experiments (e.g., button-pressing tasks) and experience-sampling studies (in which participants are prompted to answer the same questions multiple times per day on an electronic device) often produce a separate data file for each case. When merged, these become the "tall" data files addressed in Appendix B. Other types of data, in their original state, may not be in spreadsheet form at all. Your Original Data folder may potentially include a set of Word documents (e.g., interview transcripts, essays), audio or video files, physiological records, or (scanned) handwritten answers to questions on paper. Whenever your data consists of many separate files, you should create a subfolder for each type of data and put all the individual files (labeled by ID number) inside it, as depicted in Figure 3.1. In this example, there are three Excel (.xlsx) files of questionnaire data, experience-sampling data with one comma delimited (.csv) file for

🗀 3a. Original Data

    🗋 September questionnaires.xlsx

    🗋 January questionnaires.xlsx

    🗋 May questionnaires.xlsx

    🗀 Experience-sampling data

        🗋 101.csv

        🗋 102.csv

        🗋 103.csv

        (etc.)

    🗀 Interview transcripts (locked folder)

        🗋 101.docx

        🗋 102.docx

        🗋 103.docx

        (etc.)

Figure 3.1

Original data.

each participant, and interview transcripts (.docx) with one file for each participant. In this example, the interview transcripts are kept encrypted with password protection because even though access to the project folder is limited to the researchers working on the project and no participant information is attached to the data, the transcripts of interviews in a participant's own words may be sensitive enough to warrant additional protection.

Source Data and Metadata Folder

If you are obtaining your data from another source rather than collecting it yourself, you would store untouched, read-only copies of the data files you obtain in a folder called *Source Data*. Note that some projects might use source data instead of original data, whereas other projects might use both types of data. (For example, if you had permission to conduct follow-up interviews with participants from a study done 30 years ago, the interview data you collect would be original data, whereas the old data set would be source data.) Because it is relatively rare for original research projects in psychology to include source data, you probably do not have to use a Source Data folder. But if your project does include source data, see the special requirements for storing information about your source files in Appendix A.

Data for Processing Folder

Your *Data for Processing* folder will contain one or more read-only data files in SPSS format (.sav). The contents of these data files should be the same as the original data (and/or source data) files on which they are based. If your data files were already in SPSS, files in your Data for Processing folder might simply be duplicate copies of those. Note that whereas your Original/Source Data folder may include Word documents and audio or visual files, and so forth, your Data for Processing folder includes only SPSS data files. For instance, if you code (rate) a set of videotapes to capture how many times each participant nodded their head during a conversation, you could enter these codes into a spread-sheet (as described in Appendix C) and import the spreadsheet into SPSS (as described in Appendix E). The resulting SPSS file of head-nod data would then be stored in your Data for Processing folder, but the original videos files or Excel data entry files would not.

Analysis Data Folder

You must leave your Original/Source Data and Data for Processing files alone; you should not alter them or risk messing them up. Therefore, when doing data management and analysis, you will always make and use a work-ing copy of your data file(s) in the Working Data subfolder of Working Files. You can keep data files in-progress in your Working Data files folder if you want to; this is especially helpful when it takes you multiple data analysis sessions to obtain all your results. But don't forget that, because nothing in them is irreplaceable, the files in this folder are essentially temporary. At any time, you could recreate one of these files by starting over with a fresh copy of the relevant Data for Processing file and running your data management commands on it.

The larger and more complex your data set is, the more inconvenient it gets to keep repeating your data management commands whenever you want to run an analysis. It therefore makes sense to save a copy of your data file with the labeling, cleaning, and variable computation steps already done. If you want to save ready-to-analyze files, create an optional *Analysis Data* folder to store them. Save the files with informative names, and if you have many of them, use subfolders to organize them. You can always recreate an Analysis Data file using your Data for Processing file(s) and the relevant data management commands, but sometimes it is nice not to have to.

Let us imagine that you have a labeled and cleaned data set in which you have already computed the scale scores for 30 different personality variables. Saving this file in the Analysis Data folder means you will not have to recompute those scores every time you want to analyze them. For your convenience, you may even want to save a read-only file called "Computed Personality Variables" in the Analysis Data folder that contains just the 30 computed scores (and not the hundreds of individual items you used to compute them). Then, when you want to analyze the computed scores, start by putting a copy of your Analysis Data file in the Working Data folder so the Analysis Data file containing your final scale computations is left untouched for safekeeping.

GUIDELINES FOR CREATING DATA FILES

The ID Variable

Every data file will include a variable called *ID* or something comparable, indicating the case, subject, or participant from which the data came. The ID variable should be numeric, and every ID number should clearly identify a unique (different) case. This is important: Check carefully when writing or typing ID numbers, and never take chances on reusing ID numbers or switching them around after the fact. For example, if the participant to whom you gave ID number 19 suddenly became ill and left without finishing the most important parts of your study, you might not be able to use any of their data. However, you should not give a different participant ID number 19. Having two 19s in your records could cause substantial problems: Computer programs (like SPSS) may have trouble distinguishing between the two and mix them up. People working with the data set may also be confused.

Not only does it cause problems to reuse or switch ID numbers but also there are no benefits to it. When you are analyzing your data, it will not matter at all whether the ID numbers in your final sample go from 18 to 20, skipping 19. In fact, it does not matter at all what the ID numbers are—they could be a random series of values such as 9, 12, 245, 834, 631587. All that matters is eliminating any possible confusion about which case is which. Some students feel tempted to reuse or switch ID numbers because they want the IDs to reflect an accurate count of how many participants with complete, usable data they have in their sample. But this is not a chance worth taking. You can use a log file to count your participants (or to keep track of how many are in each condition) without risking major errors in your data.

Data Entry

Data entry—the process of typing information obtained on paper into a computer spreadsheet—used to be a necessary and time-consuming part of research. Fortunately, technology has reduced the amount of it you have to do. Anytime you are considering having a participant or experimenter record something on paper, think about whether they could directly enter the information into a computer instead. This will save a lot of effort and eliminate the risk of a discrepancy between the on-paper response and the one entered for analysis. With so many data collection programs available, including free online programs, there is often no need for paper forms. Collecting your data by computer and requiring a response to each item before the program can proceed will also eliminate the common problem of accidentally skipped items. Because feeling forced to answer questions can be stressful, you should consider offering "choose not to answer" as a possible response if you are going to require an answer for each question, though.

If you do have a need for data entry, though, keep in mind that you will have to enter every single response on the paper document, not just the participant's total score. To illustrate: if you gave your participants a 22-item anxiety scale, you'd enter the responses to each of the 22 items into the data file, and use SPSS commands to compute the participant's total anxiety scores. Why? Computing scales in SPSS (rather than by hand) produces a clear record of how each score was obtained—and this is exactly what you need. In addition, psychology research typically requires more information than participants' total scores. For example, you have to report the internal consistency reliability coefficient (alpha) of the scale; to find that out, you have to have in the computer not just the participants' total scores but also their answers to every individual question. You'll find instructions for computing scales and analyzing their reliability in Chapter 4.

Beyond this, every single response on paper has to be entered not once, but twice: double-entering data is necessary to prevent careless data-entry errors. Assuming that everyone on your project has promised to be careful, why should you plan ahead for careless errors? The fact is that careful people make all kinds of errors during data entry: You name it, I've seen it. Because you can't make the people on your research team be other than human, you need double-entry to prevent normal human error from interfering with the progress of science.

The logic behind double-entering data is that two people independently entering the same data will not make the same errors. A comparison of their entered data should, therefore, reveal all the errors they make so you can correct them. That process is called *data reconciliation*. If your project requires data entry, step-by-step procedures for double entering and reconciling your data are provided in Appendix C.

Naming Variables

At what point you get to name your variables will depend on how you are obtaining your data. In some situations, you'll be able to give your variables the names you want from the beginning. In other situations, your variables will be automatically given names that you'll later change. But even if you will not be assigning names to your variables right away, you should give some thought to how you want to eventually name them.

When choosing variable names, be concise and consistent. (You'll use variable labels to record the detailed information that will not fit in a short variable name, as described in Chapter 4 and Appendix D.) SPSS requires that variable names start with a letter and be free of spaces, but capitalization does not matter. Some people like to use underscores to indicate spaces in variable names (e.g., "self_esteem").

If you are administering a questionnaire consisting of multiple items, name each item with a short prefix that refers in a sensible way to the questionnaire, followed by an item number. For example, a set of questions from a depression inventory might be named dep1, dep2, dep3, and so forth; a set of questions about self-esteem might be named se1, se2, se3, and so forth. If you are using a questionnaire developed by someone else, it is a good idea to keep the item numbers the same as on the original questionnaire when you can; otherwise, people familiar with the measure in its standard form may get confused.

When naming a variable that reflects several categories, the name should refer to the overall set of categories, rather than to a single category in particular (e.g., "race"). When naming a single (stand-alone) item that has only two options, it's helpful if the name consistently reflects the higher-numbered option. For example, a variable asking, "Have you ever been enrolled in college?" with answers 0 = no and 1 = yes may sensibly be called "college." But if the answer choices had been 1 = yes and 2 = no, the variable would be more clearly identified by a name like "nocollege" to keep the meaning of the name consistent with the higher-numbered option. You may have to think ahead to design the answer choices for your study questions to be consistent with the variable names you will ultimately use.

Similarly, when naming variables that involve rating scales, use names consistent with the meaning of higher scores. A scale involving ratings of your self-esteem from *low* (1) to *high* (10) could be called something like "selfesteem," "sesteem," or "se," but a scale involving ratings of how much you experience low self-esteem (from 1 to 10) should be called "lowse" (or "lse," etc.).

The reason for these guidelines is to make it easier for you and others to make sense of your results. For instance, if you found that the variable "college" was positively correlated with the variable "se," you would be able to readily interpret this to mean that going to college was associated with higher rather than lower self-esteem. (Note that you would have to interpret this positive correlation completely differently if either of the variables were named in the direction opposite to their scores, with higher numbers signifying never having gone to college or having lower self-esteem).

Because your Original/Source Data and Data for Processing files must contain your data sets as they looked when first obtained, you should not change the variable names in these files, even if a computer program automatically gave your variables names that are not concise, consistent, or informative. Procedures for renaming variables will be covered in the section on using command files to manage your data (see Chapter 4).

CONCLUDING COMMENTS

This chapter focused on creating and preserving original data files, which are really the heart of any empirical research project. Setting up your data sets carefully (e.g., in your choice of variable names) will help you analyze them more easily, too.

4

Your Command Files

Command files are one of the types of files used by statistical packages such as SPSS, along with data files and output files. SPSS refers
to command files as *syntax* and gives them the file extension ".sps."
Command files start out as blank windows, but you fill them with the
commands used for everything you do with your data—from data management tasks (importing and merging data files, renaming, cleaning,
labeling, and computing variables) to conducting statistical analyses.
Because they serve as readily reusable records of everything you do, command files are the central documentation your project needs. But command files are not just good for your project records and others looking
at your work—they are also good for you. They can be created in advance,
before you even have all your data ready to analyze, thus reducing the

http://dx.doi.org/10.1037/0000068-004
Managing Your Research Data and Documentation, by K. R. Berenson
Copyright © 2018 by the American Psychological Association. All rights reserved.

time crunch that may occur if you are working under a deadline. They can be used at the touch of a button, as many times as necessary, and are easily modified. If after you do an analysis, you misplace your output, you get more data, or you realize there is something you want to do differently (e.g., control for another variable or exclude a participant who did not follow directions), a command file will allow you to repeat your analyses in minutes. The point-and-click method of using SPSS, however, would have you starting over from scratch in these situations—maybe putting you in a state of panic if you're under time pressure or if you're having trouble recreating exactly what you did before. Command files take a lot of the stress out of working with data because they make everything easily re-doable and fixable.

Some students are reluctant to use command files because they find the idea intimidating, as if it were a kind of computer programming. If that's how you're thinking about this process, you're making way too much of it, and rather than develop a pattern of fearful avoidance, you should push yourself to start using command files as soon and as often as you can. Those who regularly teach students to use command files for data documentation and analysis have observed that even students who expect to hate this approach eventually come to appreciate it. It helps students analyze their data with more efficiency and organization and makes it easier for professors to give them useful feedback. It removes the pressure to get results from a fresh, raw data set in a single rushed lab session that will barely be remembered as a blur of anxious clicks and instead gives students the experience of handling data in ways that are compatible with planning, thoughtfulness, and accountability. Ultimately, students who learn to work with data this way appear to gain a deeper and more confident understanding of their research, as well as a greater understanding of what it means to uphold our ethical responsibilities as psychological scientists (Ball & Medeiros, 2012). This chapter begins with an explanation of why command files are the easiest and most accurate way to document your research. It then provides a basic overview of command files in SPSS.

COMMAND FILES MAKE THE BEST
RESEARCH DOCUMENTATION

Why Command Files Make Better
Documentation Than Output

Students who do not like the idea of creating command files sometimes try to argue that they can accomplish the same thing by saving their output—after all, the output shows everything they did, right? Well, yes and no. First, output files are cumbersome. If you work on SPSS for a little while, you will soon accumulate hundreds of pages of output. No one wants to have to look through all that output just to find answers to simple questions about your data set and analyses—and they should not have to. Second, what people need to verify your results is the ability to replicate what you did. Seeing the numbers on your output isn't sufficient—they have to be able to run analyses with your data and get those numbers themselves.

It is true that SPSS includes executed commands in the output, so it would be technically possible for you to cut and paste the commands from your output file into a command file. But digging through your output to cut and paste is not going to be the easiest way for you to create a command file. You are better off creating the command file as you go.

Why Command Files Make Better Documentation
Than Typed Lists and Descriptions

Chances are that if you've ever been taught about data management, that lesson somehow involved a large loose-leaf book called a study manual (guide, codebook, etc.), full of typed documents. Loose-leaf books of this sort can be useful, and you can easily create one by printing out some of the files you will store in your project folder on your computer. However, one major section of the loose-leaf project book ought to be omitted— the typed documents describing your variables. You should use command files to serve this purpose instead.

Researchers used to put a lot of effort into typing up descriptions of variables. For example, if your research used a questionnaire measuring a personality trait such as extraversion, you would have created a document listing all the items included in your extraversion scale and the formula for how the total score was calculated so that this polished document could be relied on as the definitive source of information about the extraversion measure in your study. But this procedure had drawbacks. First, it required a lot of unnecessary effort: Instead of using one document to describe your extraversion scale (the commands used to create it), this procedure created two. Second, because this procedure involved documenting the same information twice, it introduced an unnecessary risk for making an error or omission in one place or the other, and this risk would markedly increase over time for longer term projects. Eventually, someone would likely discover that the information in the two documents was no longer the same and that relying on the fancy typed-up description had been causing confusion and errors. You can avoid problems and do less work by only creating and updating the one document you need, which is the SPSS command file. Just make the command file as user-friendly and information rich as the typed document would have been by putting the explanatory details directly in there, in variable labels and comments.

Projects vary a lot in terms of how many command files they require. Some projects can sensibly fit all their commands into one file; others use so many command files that subfolders are required to keep them organized. If your project uses more than one command file, give them names that distinguish what they do. For example, a project might use two files called "Managing Data" and "Analyzing Data." A project in which the Original/Source Data files were not in SPSS and first had to be imported (see Appendix E) is likely to require an additional command file; it might be named "Creating the Data for Processing Files." A project requiring many different command files may have separate ones for different data management tasks and different analyses, with more detailed names such as "Computing Anxiety Scales" or "Correlations With Personality Variables" or "Analyses Comparing 2 Groups."

GETTING ACQUAINTED WITH
COMMAND FILES IN SPSS

Whenever the SPSS application is open, you will have a data file window open on your screen, either blank or containing data. Output files automatically appear whenever you run analyses or other operations on your data file. By contrast, SPSS won't put a command file on your screen unless you ask for one (by opening an existing command file or requesting a new one). To open an existing command file, use the File menu to select "Open" and "Syntax," and then choose the name of the command file you want. To open a blank command file, use the File menu to select "New" and then "Syntax."

You'll add commands to your command files with a combination of pasting and typing. If you like using the SPSS menus and dialogue boxes to work with data, you still can; the only difference is that you always click "Paste" instead of clicking "OK," so that all the commands are pasted into a command file that you can keep. New commands are always pasted at the end of your file, though you can move them afterward if you want to. To prevent SPSS from pasting commands into the wrong file, though, it is important not to have more than one command file open at the same time. You can also type directly into command files, and at a minimum, you will type informative comments (instructions, headings) to help orient a reader to the commands you include in your files. You may also find that some commands are easier to work with by typing rather than by pasting from the SPSS menus. Remember to save your command files on a regular basis while you are working with them.

To illustrate how you would use a command file simultaneously to perform and document a statistical analysis, imagine you wanted to examine the frequencies of responses to several variables from the Big Five Inventory (BFI; John, Donahue, & Kentle, 1991). If you want to use the SPSS menus for the analysis, you would click on "Analyze" and then select "Descriptive Statistics" and "Frequencies." A dialogue box would appear, and you would select which variables you would like to analyze. Then, you would click the Paste button, which is just to the right of the OK button, as shown in Figure 4.1.

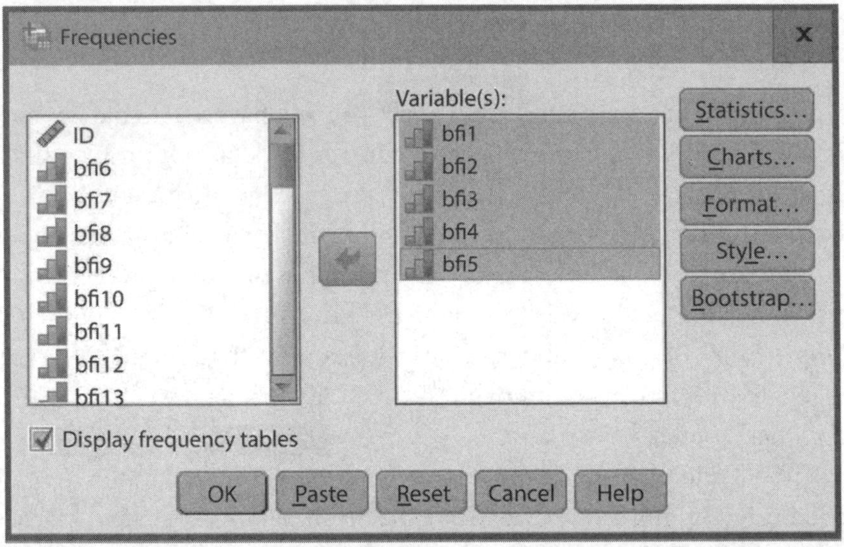

Figure 4.1

Pasting commands. From IBM SPSS Statistics, Version 24.0, by IBM Corporation, 2016, Armonk, NY: IBM Corporation. Copyright 2016 by IBM Corporation.

Now if you look at your command file, you can find the command you just pasted, at the end of the file.[1]

FREQUENCIES VARIABLES=bfi1 bfi2 bfi3 bfi4 bfi5
/ORDER=ANALYSIS.

Select or highlight the command(s) you want to run, and then click on the green forward arrow (or "play") button at the top of your screen (directly beneath the Utilities menu).

Because it's common to run the same commands on several variables at once, it can be useful to edit a command by pasting into it a list of the variables to which you would like the command to be applied. To quickly obtain such a list of variables, use the Utilities menu and click "Variables." Select or highlight the variables you want, and click the Paste button. You

---

[1]Note that although SPSS automatically pastes the specification "/ORDER=ANALYSIS" into this command, this is not necessary. It similarly does not matter whether you capitalize the command words the way SPSS does. It would be sufficient to type the command: "Frequencies bfi1 bfi2 bfi3 bfi4 bfi5."

can also copy and paste the resulting list of variable names from one part of your command file to other parts. For example, if you want to conduct frequencies analyses on some self-esteem variables, in addition to the BFI variables you have already selected, you could paste "se1 se2 se3 se4 se5 se6 se7 se8 se9 se10" into your command to modify it as follows:

FREQUENCIES VARIABLES=bfi1 bfi2 bfi3 bfi4 bfi5 se1 se2 se3 se4 se5 se6 se7 se8 se9 se10
/ORDER=ANALYSIS.

When typing commands or modifying pasted commands, remember that every command must end with a period. Often, if your command has incorrect punctuation it will be shown in unusual colors, and it will change color as soon as that issue has been corrected.

Some commands used for recoding and computing variables require an additional instruction for the command to run. Specifically, in these cases, you have to type the word EXECUTE followed by a period on the line directly beneath the command, as shown in many examples later in this chapter. However, commands used for labeling variables and analyzing data (e.g., the frequencies analysis) do not require an EXECUTE line. The fact that SPSS only sometimes requires EXECUTE lines is something to be aware of, but not something about which to worry. Extra, unnecessary EXECUTE lines are harmless; the worst they do is make your command files look a little cluttered. Similarly, omitting a necessary EXECUTE line isn't the end of the world; you'd see that your command does not run and add the missing EXECUTE line.

When your commands run successfully, you will be able to see the results of your work in your output and/or your data file. If there are problems with your commands, your output file will say so. Look for spelling errors: Computers can be frustrating in that they are not able to figure out what you meant to say if you misspelled a variable name or a word used as part of a command. Punctuation errors are similarly a big deal, such as omitting a period at the end of your command or forgetting to enclose with an asterisk and a period everything that isn't an SPSS command. If there are no error messages in your output, but your commands failed to create the new variables you requested, you are probably missing a necessary EXECUTE line. Fix any errors you can think of, and try running the command again until it works. Above all, remember that nothing you do can permanently damage your data because you are not touching the saved Data for Processing files, only working copies. Error messages aren't anything to fear—they're just problems to be solved.

To build up self-efficacy for using command files, start by creating commands using the Paste button and adding comments (as described in the next section). Then, get used to modifying pasted commands by changing or adding variables. After you are comfortable with command files, the Syntax Guide available under the Help menu in SPSS has a lot of useful information for writing customized commands. (But because this guide contains commands for zillions of SPSS procedures, it would be an overwhelming place for a beginner to start.)

Note that you can start working on command files for your project even before your data are collected. For example, if you have to compute scales, you can start right away on the commands to do that, described later in this chapter. If you like to paste commands and variable names when you create commands, a helpful tip is to use the data from one participant, maybe even a fake participant, as a model for what your eventual data files will look like when all your data are collected.

Using Comments in Command Files

Regardless of whether you create your commands by pasting, typing, or a combination of both, you should type comments before each command to help orient the reader. Each comment must start with an asterisk (*) and end with a period. Your comment will turn pale gray when your punctuation is correct for SPSS to recognize it as a comment. Comments do not need an EXECUTE line.

The top of every command file should start with a series of comments summarizing what the command file is for, identifying the name(s) and location(s) of the data file(s) that it should be used with and providing any instructions needed to use it. For example:

*Jane Doe and James Bond.
*Psych 399 group assignment due 4/3/17.
*This file is called managing data.sps.
*These commands apply labels, clean the data set, and compute scales.
*Use these commands with September Questionnaires.sav in the Data
for Processing folder.

A comment should be added right before each command to explain what the upcoming command is for. You also include optional comments after the end of your command if you would like to say anything further about it—but do not type comments in the middle of SPSS commands. Keep each comment less than one line long. If you have a lot to say, divide it up into separate short comments. You can say anything you want in comments as long as you use the proper punctuation (starting with an asterisk and ending with a period). Do not use any periods inside a comment, or SPSS will interpret the period as ending the comment.

Absolutely everything in your command file must be either a command or a comment, or else SPSS will think it is a mistake and give you an error message. This means that if you want to put your name on the top of your command file, you have to put it in a comment. If you want to note the date on which you did particular analyses, put the date in a comment. If you want to add headings to divide your command file into organized sections, you have to do that using comments. The following are some common types of comments (you'll see more examples throughout the rest of the book):

*Frequencies analysis for big five and self-esteem variables.
*Assigning value labels for the demographics questionnaire.
*Setting "refuse to answer" responses as missing.
*Computing scales for the Big Five Inventory (BFI).
*ANOVA reported on page 6 of paper.

Making Command Files Easy to Access

Although the SPSS application is necessary to run command files and to paste material from SPSS menus into them, the contents of command files can be saved, read, and edited as ordinary text in a Word document. There may be times when you want to open your command files on a computer that does not have SPSS; you can do that if you regularly save them that way. Choose "Select All" on the upper right of your command file window, copy, and paste the entire selection into a Word document, then save it in your Command Files folder, with the same file name and a .docx extension.

You are strongly encouraged to save the final versions of your command files as PDFs for an easily accessible, permanent record of your work. Depending on your computer system, you may be able to do this by selecting either "Export" (right click on your command file window to see this) or "Print" (on the File menu).

USING COMMAND FILES FOR DATA MANAGEMENT AND ANALYSIS

Next, we cover the steps you will take to get your results, starting with your original data files. First will come data management tasks, such as putting an SPSS data set together, applying labels to it, and cleaning it. Then you will compute variables for your analyses by combining existing variables into scales and/or otherwise recoding them. Finally, you will conduct analyses to test your hypotheses. Although not all of these steps are likely to be an explicit focus of your paper, they are all important and can have a substantial influence on your results. Using command files to carry out each step will ensure that every decision you make with your data is completely documented and reproducible, from the beginning.

Creating and Managing Your Data for Processing Files

Your Data for Processing files are SPSS versions of your original data. If your original data are already in an SPSS data set, all you have to do is copy it. Many other types of data files (e.g., SAS, Excel) can also be opened by SPSS and saved in that format, without a need to formally import them. If you do need to import and/or merge data files, see Appendices E and F for instructions, and be sure to save the commands you use.

Next, you will perform data management tasks and data analyses on working copies of your Data for Processing files. You'll begin by saving a copy of the data set that you want to use into your Working Files folder, so that you never modify the saved Data for Processing file itself. The remainder of this chapter and the accompanying appendices provide instructions for many of the most common procedures you'll need for data management and analysis. These procedures are all listed in the index at the back of the book, for your reference.

Renaming Variables

If your variables were automatically assigned names that are long, confusing, uninformative, or otherwise hard to work with, you will use commands to rename them. Put each old variable name and new variable name together in parentheses as follows:

*Giving variables shorter names.
RENAME VARIABLES (Youidentifyyourselfas=gender).
RENAME VARIABLES (Yourageinyears=age).

If you have a lot of variables to rename at once, you can use the data manager's tip described in Appendix D to create a lot of variable renaming commands quickly and efficiently.

Assigning Variable Labels

Because SPSS variable names are meant to be short, they do not leave much room for detailed explanation. Variable labels are therefore useful to give more specific information. For survey questions, one option is to include the actual wording of each item in your variable label. Another popular option is to use a short phrase summarizing the essential meaning of the item, rather than the actual wording. For example, if your research project includes an anxiety questionnaire in which the sixth question, named anx6, is "How often do you have a shaky voice?" a useful variable label for anx6 might be "How often do you have a shaky voice?" or it might be "Shaky voice."

Using the exact wording of the item is often the fastest way to assign variable labels because you can copy and paste the wording right out of the questionnaire rather than having to think about how to summarize it. Labels containing the exact wording can also reduce the need to look up the wording on the original questionnaires while interpreting your results. However, using shorter labels that get straight to the point of the item can make your output easier to read. In addition, if your study includes items whose content has copyright restrictions, including the full text of these items in your variable labels will mean that you will have to remove or modify these labels when creating your publicly shareable Replication Documentation folder (see Chapter 5). Use the labels that make the most sense for your project; you may want to use exact wording for some items and shorter summaries for other items. Don't use quotation marks or apostrophes in your labels because SPSS finds this confusing. You may want to use a search command to find and remove all of them systematically.

Some students have learned to assign variable labels and value labels by typing and pasting into the appropriate boxes using the "Variable View" tab on the SPSS data window, and this approach may sometimes be appropriate for small, short-term projects. However, because SPSS does not give you the option to paste and save procedures on the Variable View tab as reusable commands (at least as of SPSS Version 24), it is far better to use command language for these tasks instead. It is especially important to use command language to label variables for long-term projects (for which data files are likely to be updated multiple times) or when you will be switching back and forth between various computer packages and formats (e.g., SAS, R, Excel). Converting data files often erases the labels, and you should have the commands ready to put them back on.

To use command language to assign variable labels, use a separate command line for each variable, as shown in the following example. Each command includes the words VARIABLE LABEL, the variable name, the label in quotes, and a period. No EXECUTE line is necessary. The following are the commands you would use to label the first five items of the BFI:

*Assigning variable labels to the Big Five Inventory (BFI) items.
*Note that each item starts with "I see myself as someone who".

VARIABLE LABEL bfi1 'is talkative'.
VARIABLE LABEL bfi2 'tends to find fault in others'.
VARIABLE LABEL bfi3 'does a thorough job'.
VARIABLE LABEL bfi4 'is depressed, blue'.
VARIABLE LABEL bfi5 'is original, comes up with new ideas'.

If you have a lot of variables to label at once, you can create the commands quickly using the data manager's tip shown in Appendix D.

Assigning Value Labels

Value labels are used to keep track of what your response options mean. There is no need to include value labels when the response is self-explanatory (e.g., your age in years, what percentage of the time are you shy). However, you should always include value labels for items such as participant gender because it is otherwise all too easy to lose track of which responses were which. The following is an example of the commands you would use to assign value labels to BFI items. Because all the items on this scale use the same set of response options, you can assign them all value labels at once by pasting the entire list of variable names into the command (as previously described). Notice how the punctuation works—with a period only at the end of the entire command. An EXECUTE line is not necessary.

> *Assigning value labels to the Big Five Inventory (BFI) response options.
> VALUE LABELS bfi1 bfi2 bfi3 bfi4 bfi5 bfi6 bfi7 bfi8 bfi9 bfi10 bfi11 bfi12 bfi13 bfi14 bfi15 bfi16 bfi17 bfi18 bfi19 bfi20 bfi21 bfi22 bfi23 bfi24 bfi25 bfi26 bfi27 bfi28 bfi29 bfi30 bfi31 bfi32 bfi33 bfi34 bfi35 bfi36 bfi37 bfi38 bfi39 bfi40 bfi41 bfi42 bfi43 bfi44
> 1 'disagree strongly'
> 2 'disagree a little'
> 3 'neither agree nor disagree'
> 4 'agree a little'
> 5 'agree strongly'
> 6 'refuse to answer'.

Checking Frequency Tables for Data Errors

Frequencies analyses can be useful for spotting problems in your data before you proceed with more complex computations and analyses. First, make sure there are no impossible values. For example, because items from the BFI were rated on a 1-to-5 scale (with 6 for *refuse to answer*), there should not be any 8s. Likewise, the ages of participants from a college sample should not (usually) show that anyone is 9 years old or 194 years old. If you find impossible values, try to figure out what went wrong. Maybe a participant's handwriting was confusing enough to be misinterpreted by both people who entered the data. Or a participant carelessly typed that they were 9 years old instead of 19. If you can tell what the correct answer ought to be, write commands to make the corrections using comments to explain the reason for each change.

> *Cleaning the data set.
> *Correcting data errors.
> *132's handwriting was misread; bfi4 score should be a 3, not an 8.
> IF ID=132 bfi4=3.
> *Typo in 276; participant was a college student and not age 9; best guess is age 19.
> IF ID=276 age=19.
> EXECUTE.

If you ever make corrections that involve any guesswork whatsoever, you should directly admit this in your command file (as in the earlier example). But it is rare to make corrections such as this because doing so is only appropriate under particular circumstances. If participant age were a central variable of interest in your study, it would be problematic to include participants whose age was not 100% certain or to make a "guess" about a participant's age that could influence your hypothesis testing one way or the other. However, the guess made in the previous example would be completely appropriate for a study of college students that has nothing to do with age differences. (Here, the age variable only comes in to play when reporting descriptive statistics on the sample—there is no chance that the participant was really 9 years old, and the correct age is going to be close to 19 anyway.)

Most important is to remember that no corrections are ever made to your saved original or source data or data for processing, even when the corrections involve no guesses and seem (in your opinion) completely uncontroversial. Instead, use your command file to make all corrections to your Working Data file and include comments to explain and justify the changes you make.

Using Missing Data Codes

In your frequencies analyses, make sure the sample size is always the same as your total sample size. In other words, every case should have a value for every variable, with those who did not provide data for a particular question not being left blank, but instead receiving an appropriate missing data code. When questions are skipped in computerized data collection programs, they are often automatically assigned a value of 99 or 999. When researchers enter data into spreadsheets, they should likewise use missing data codes rather than leave columns blank. If for any reason your data do not have the same sample size for every case, you can set the blank columns to be 99 (or some other specified value) using "Recode into Same Variables" on the Transform menu. If you did this for all 44 items on the BFI, your command would look something like this:

> *Setting empty columns to be 99 for the Big Five Inventory (BFI).
> RECODE bfi1 bfi2 bfi3 bfi4 bfi5 bfi6 bfi7 bfi8 bfi9 bfi10 bfi11 bfi12
> bfi13 bfi14 bfi15 bfi16 bfi17 bfi18 bfi19 bfi20 bfi21 bfi22 bfi23 bfi24
> bfi25 bfi26 bfi27 bfi28 bfi29 bfi30 bfi31 bfi32 bfi33 bfi34 bfi35 bfi36
> bfi37 bfi38 bfi39 bfi40 bfi41 bfi42 bfi43 bfi44 (MISSING=99).
> EXECUTE.

If after running this command you did a frequencies analysis, you would have values for every single case for every single BFI item, as you should; there would be no blank columns. This is good as a first step. But next you have to specify that the 99 values are not actual answers, but just missing data codes.

To illustrate, consider a questionnaire that asks for participants' relationship status and then, "If you are currently involved in a relationship, how many years have you been together?" Participants who are single will appropriately leave the second question (named "yrsrel") blank, and their blank answer will end up being recorded in the data file with a missing data code such as 99. To do analyses on the duration of the relationships in your study, it would be important not to accidentally include these 99s as if they meant the single participants had been in relationships lasting 99 years. Instead, you should tell SPSS to understand that 99 means the data are missing and should be ignored so that your analysis of relationship duration will only include people who are in relationships. To paste the commands for this procedure into your command file, go to "Recode into Same Variables" under the Transform menu, select the variable(s) you want to recode, specify that the old value 99 should be recoded as system missing (SYSMIS), and click the paste button.

```
*Setting 99 values as missing data codes for relationship duration.
RECODE yrsrel (99=SYSMIS).
EXECUTE.
```

For another example, the following is how you could indicate that for all the items from the BFI, values of 99 and 6 should both be counted as missing (for the reasons explained in the comments introducing the command):

```
*Setting 99 and 6 values as missing data codes for the Big Five Inventory (BFI).
*Note that blank answers were coded 99 and 6 was the "refuse to answer" option.
RECODE bfi1 bfi2 bfi3 bfi4 bfi5 bfi6 bfi7 bfi8 bfi9 bfi10 bfi11 bfi12 bfi13 bfi14 bfi15 bfi16 bfi17 bfi18 bfi19 bfi20 bfi21 bfi22 bfi23 bfi24 bfi25 bfi26 bfi27 bfi28 bfi29 bfi30 bfi31 bfi32 bfi33 bfi34 bfi35 bfi36 bfi37 bfi38 bfi39 bfi40 bfi41 bfi42 bfi43 bfi44 (99=SYSMIS) (6=SYSMIS).
EXECUTE.
```

Handling Missing Data

At this point in the data cleaning process you have ensured that blank responses are marked with a missing data code and that SPSS understands that these codes signify missing data rather than real numeric answers. This is all you have to do for items that are not applicable and therefore supposed to be missing. But sometimes data are missing for more unfortunate reasons. Study administration problems can result in questions being unasked. For example, did the participant not finish the whole study? Were portions somehow omitted due to a computer error or copy machine malfunction? Skipping an item by accident is also common, and unless you put measures in place to prevent or discourage participants from carelessly omitting random items, you should expect to lose a lot of data this way. Finally, deliberately choosing to skip particular items is common, especially for items that are personal or sensitive, unclear, or complicated. When information is missing for reasons such as these, deciding what to do about it takes careful thought.

Consider an example of a research project in which you gave participants a 20-item questionnaire about whether they had recently engaged in disordered eating behaviors such as binge eating or deliberately vomiting after meals. For each question, then, your data file would contain a "0" if the participant answered "no," a "1" if the participant answered "yes," and a missing data code such as "99" if the participant left the question blank. Because the authors of this questionnaire instruct you to use the total (sum) of the items answered "yes" as the participant's total score (such that higher scores indicate more problems with disordered eating), each participant should end up with a score between 0 (saying "no" to all the questions) and 20 (saying "yes" to all the questions). As in the previous example (about the duration of participants' relationships), you should use the RECODE command to set 99 scores as system missing (SYSMIS). But unlike that example, you cannot just ignore the missing answers as if they were not applicable. If you tell SPSS to regard the 99 scores as missing and just take the sum of the scores that the participant did answer, you are ostensibly counting the missing scores as if they were answered "no." Someone who refused to answer nearly the entire questionnaire might be erroneously scored as having no eating disordered behavior whatsoever, in spite of the fact that they did not say "no" to those questions. Though you will never know what the missing answers to those questions were, you certainly cannot just assume all the missing answers were "no." How should you handle cases that are missing information (where it is not supposed to be missing)? Should you exclude them? Estimate the missing values? Do something else?

Because your decisions depend, in part, on the magnitude of the problem (how much data are missing), you may want to have a systematic way to determine that. You can create a variable that counts, for each case, how many values are missing from a specified set of items. (You can paste this command by clicking "Compute Variable" on the Transform menu.) Give your new variable a name that indicates what it does. In this example, you are creating a variable to count how many items are missing from the BFI and calling it "cmiss_bfi," with cmiss being an abbreviation for "count missing." Because there are 44 items, the new variable will range from 0 to 44.

> *Determining how many items are missing from the Big Five Inventory (BFI).
> COUNT cmiss_bfi=bfi1 bfi2 bfi3 bfi4 bfi5 bfi6 bfi7 bfi8 bfi9 bfi10 bfi11 bfi12 bfi13 bfi14 bfi15 bfi16 bfi17 bfi18 bfi19 bfi20 bfi21 bfi22 bfi23 bfi24 bfi25 bfi26 bfi27 bfi28 bfi29 bfi30 bfi31 bfi32 bfi33 bfi34 bfi35 bfi36 bfi37 bfi38 bfi39 bfi40 bfi41 bfi42 bfi43 bfi44 (SYSMIS).
> EXECUTE.
> VARIABLE LABEL cmiss_bfi 'count number of items missing from Big Five Inventory'.

A frequencies analysis on cmiss_bfi will then show you how many cases may have a substantial problem with missing data for the BFI measure. To identify which specific participants are missing items, you could use the "Sort Cases" command (in the Data menu) to sort the cases on cmiss_bfi, or you could run a crosstabs of cmiss_bfi and ID (Descriptive Statistics, Crosstabs on the Analysis menu).

Estimating a missing value (as described in Appendix G) is relatively easy to justify if it plays no part in your hypothesis and/or if it is just one randomly missing item contributing to a multiple-item scale. However, when more information is missing, and when that information is essential to your results, estimation becomes harder to justify. In addition, if the participant's omission of a response was deliberate (rather than accidental or coincidental), you may find yourself left without any reasonable basis for making an estimate. Sometimes you have no choice but to exclude the case.[2]

But why go to this trouble and not just always exclude cases with missing data? There are good reasons to try to keep as many cases as you can. One reason is practical—collecting data can take a lot of time and money, especially with complex study designs and carefully selected samples, so researchers are often reluctant to discard data unless it is necessary. An even better reason to try to keep all your cases is to maximize the generalizability of your research findings. Is it not normal and expected that participants will sometimes make errors, be uncomfortable answering particular questions, or be absent from a study session, and so on? Restricting your research sample to participants who provide complete and perfect data may make it less representative of the population you are studying.

The correct solution for handling your missing data depends on the circumstances, including how much data is missing, how essential it is to your study, and whether you have the basis for making a good estimate that will not bias your study results. Whatever you decide to do has to be carefully thought through, justified, and documented in your command files as well as in your Data Issues log.

Excluding Cases

If cases need to be excluded (according to your Data Issues log), you must never just delete them from your Original Data or Data for Processing files because there has to be a clear record of these decisions in your command

---

[2]It can be problematic to estimate an item that a participant refused to answer from items that the participant willingly answered because the only thing you know for sure about the refused item is that the participant considered it different from all the answerable ones. If items that participants frequently refuse to answer are an essential focus of your study, splitting your sample into groups may be a good alternative to having to exclude a lot of cases. In the case of the disordered eating questionnaire, you could use the published scale norms to define a group that is high in disordered eating symptoms (above a particular cutoff) and a group that is low in disordered eating symptoms (below a particular cutoff). This way, participants who refused to answer a few items could still be included in one of these groups, as long as they would still fit in that group no matter what their missing answers were. Certainly, participants who omitted so many items that you cannot even determine which group they would be in would still have to be excluded from your sample. But often you will have enough information to know which group a participant is in, even when missing items prevent you from definitively knowing his or her actual score.

files. The way you do this is to create a variable that identifies the cases needing exclusion and then run a command that uses this variable to select the cases you want.

Imagine you wanted to exclude two specific cases, ID numbers 102 and 199, from your analyses. The following is a portion of a command file that would allow you to do that. Notice that you are first setting all the cases to have an exclude score of 0 and then specifying which cases ought to have scores other than 0. You could type these commands or paste them by clicking "Compute Variable" on the Transform menu.

> *Creating a variable for excluding specific participants from analyses.
> COMPUTE exclude=0.
> IF ID=102 exclude=1.
> IF ID=199 exclude=1.
> EXECUTE.
> VARIABLE LABEL exclude 'exclude participant from analyses'.

To indicate the reason why you have decided to exclude a case, you can insert an explanatory comment into your command file, such as

> *Case 102 excluded due to experimenter/equipment error.

When you are excluding more than a couple of cases, it will make more sense to document your exclusion reasons systematically by giving your exclude variable value labels that code the reasons into categories. This way you will be able to conduct a frequencies analysis on your exclude variable to facilitate reporting in your paper the number of cases you excluded for various reasons. For example,

> *Values of "exclude" indicate general categories of reasons for exclusion.
> VALUE LABELS exclude
> 0 'do not exclude'
> 1 'exclude because of experimenter/equipment error'
> 2 'exclude because missing essential data'
> 3 'exclude because didn't meet eligibility requirements'
> 4 'exclude because didn't properly complete procedures'.

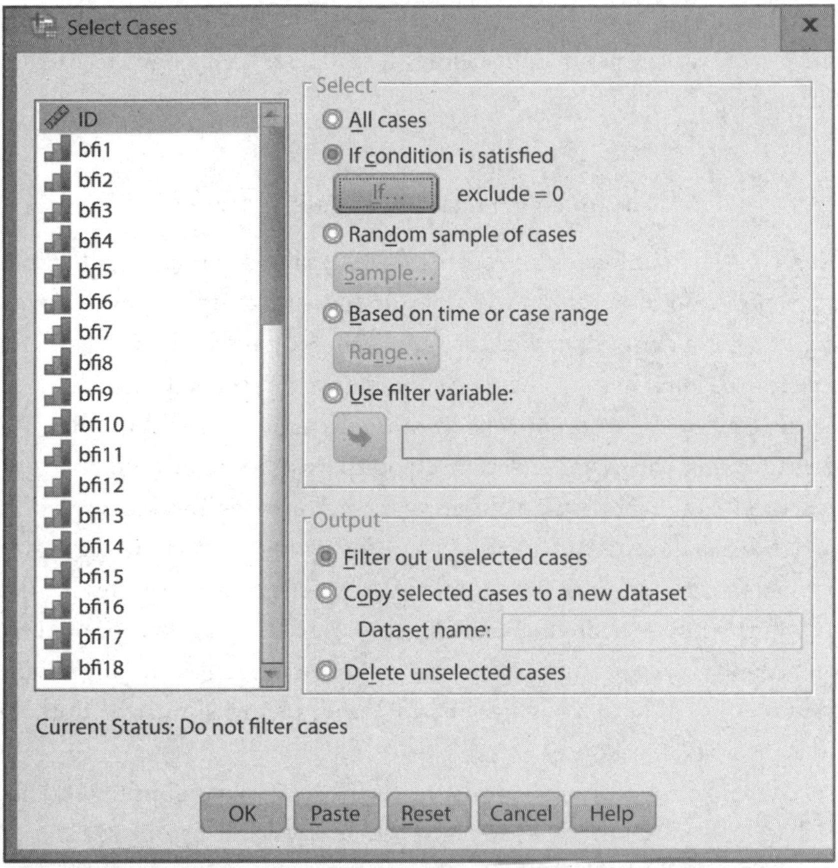

Figure 4.2

Select Cases. From IBM SPSS Statistics, Version 24.0, by IBM Corporation, 2016, Armonk, NY: IBM Corporation. Copyright 2016 by IBM Corporation.

To use your exclude variable to select cases, go to "Select Cases," under the Data menu. Choose "If condition is satisfied" and put exclude=0 in the dialogue box shown in Figure 4.2. What you choose next depends on whether you want to exclude the same cases from all of your analyses or just some of them. One option is to permanently delete the excluded cases from your Working Data file (or Analysis Data file); to do this, you would choose "Delete unselected cases" for the output choice. Another option is to keep the cases in your data set but exclude them from particular analyses; to do this, choose "Filter out unselected cases" and run this command right before the analyses that ought to exclude the cases.

Computing Variables: Recoding Items

To recode an item means to rescore it by reversing or otherwise changing its response options. As you will see from the upcoming examples, recoding items is a common procedure in psychology research. The essential rule for recoding items is that you should give the recoded variable a new name, leaving the original version of the variable alone. Why? Because if you change the original variable, you may lose track of which way it is scored, and every time you run your commands the scoring could switch back and forth. This can be confusing and will eventually cause errors. To clarify, it is OK to recode missing values (to indicate they are missing) without changing the variable name, as described previously, because specifying your missing data code does not substantially change the meaning of your variable. But any other changes must be done by creating a new variable.

When you are doing a straightforward reversal or simple recoding of a variable, it is customary to name the new variable by putting an *r* on the end of the old name. The variable label for the new variable should also clearly indicate that the item is reversed or recoded, to avoid confusion. For example, imagine you administered an anxiety questionnaire in which participants rated a series of statements from 1 (*not at all like me*) to 7 (*very much like me*). Some of the statements are phrased so that high scores indicate high anxiety ("I am a very anxious person") and some are backward, with high scores indicating low anxiety ("I never feel any anxiety whatsoever"). Backward-phrased items are commonly used because they help capture variability on both ends of a dimension and reduce the influence of response biases (the tendency to give high ratings to statements in general). You should reverse the backward items when computing participants' anxiety scores, and if the original backward item was named anx2, you could name the new reversed item anx2r. The following command could be typed or pasted from the "Recode into Different Variables" command under the Transform menu.

*Reversing backward anxiety scale items.
RECODE anx2 INTO anx2r (1=7) (2=6) (3=5) (4=4) (5=3) (6=2) (7=1).
EXECUTE.
VARIABLE LABEL anx2r 'REV-I never feel any anxiety whatsoever'.

This simpler "Compute Variable" command (also under the Transform menu) would also accomplish the same thing. (Do the math and you will see how: For example, if anx2 = 5, then anx2r would be 8 − 5 or 3.)

*Reversing backward anxiety scale items.
COMPUTE anx2r=8-anx2.
EXECUTE.
VARIABLE LABEL anx2r 'REV-I never feel any anxiety whatsoever'.

As another example of recoding a variable, perhaps you asked a sample of introductory psychology students their current relationship status, and the response options were originally labeled as follows:

*Assigning value labels to the relationship status response options.
VALUE LABELS relstatus
1 'single'
2 'casual dating only'
3 'in a relationship'
4 'married or living with a relationship partner'.

Perhaps after analyzing the data, you discovered that only a few participants selected Answer 4, and for the purposes of your study it made more sense to combine Categories 3 and 4. (The new combined category would include everyone in a relationship whether they are living with their partner or not.) You could use the "Recode" command (on the Transform menu) to create a new relationship status variable named relstatr that makes this change.

*Recoding relationship status variable to have a combined "in a relationship" category.
RECODE relstat INTO relstatr (1=1) (2=2) (3=3) (4=3).
EXECUTE.
VARIABLE LABEL relstatr 'Relationship status - recoded'.

Note that the following "Compute Variable" commands (found under the Transform menu) would also work, as an alternative:

*Recoding relationship status variable to have a combined "in a relationship" category.
COMPUTE relstatr=relstat.
IF relstat=4 relstatr=3.
EXECUTE.
VARIABLE LABEL relstatr 'Relationship status - recoded'.

And of course, regardless of how you create your new variable, you would give it value labels.

*Assigning value labels to the recoded relationship status variable response options.
VALUE LABELS relstatr
1 'single'
2 'casual dating only'
3 'in a relationship or married or living with a relationship partner'.

When doing a recoding that changes the meaning of a variable, you should give your new variable a name that is informative about its content. For example, if you wanted to recode the relationship status variable from the previous example so that it identifies all the participants who said they were single, you could create a new variable called *single* using these commands.

*Creating variable to identify single participants by recoding relationship status.
IF relstat=1 single=1.
IF relstat >1 single=0.
EXECUTE.

VARIABLE LABEL single 'Participant is single'.
*Assigning value labels to the single variable response options.
VALUE LABELS single
0 'no, not single'
1 'yes, single'.

For another example, imagine you have an age variable (age) and for some reason want to group your participants by whether they are over or under 40. You would leave the age variable as is, but create a new variable you could call *over40*. You can obtain the commands for this procedure (shown next) by typing them or by pasting from "Recode into Different Variables" on the Transform menu.

*Creating variable to identify participants who are age 40+.
RECODE age INTO over40 (0 thru 39=0) (40 thru highest=1).
EXECUTE.
VARIABLE LABEL over40 'participant is 40+'.

These alternative commands would also accomplish the same thing. Note that lt = less than and ge = greater than or equal to. (Also, le = less than or equal to and gt = greater than, ne = not equal to.)

*Creating variable to identify participants who are age 40+.
IF age lt 40 over40=0.
IF age ge 40 over40=1.
EXECUTE.
VARIABLE LABEL over40 'participant is 40+'.
As always, you will supply your new variable with value labels:
VALUE LABELS over40
0 'no, participant is under 40'
1 'yes, participant is 40+'.

Variables are commonly dichotomized (split into two groups) using the same kinds of commands as the previous example, and you could easily have called your new variable *agegp* (age group) with the value labels *low age/high age* (or *younger/older*). Likewise, if you were dichotomizing an extraversion scale to split your sample into groups of relatively low extraversion participants (i.e., the more introverted ones) and high extra-version participants, you could use the same approach to split it at the variable's median (3.38) or another chosen value.

> *Creating extraversion group variable, splitting extraversion at the median.
> IF extraversion lt 3.38 extravgp=0.
> IF extraversion ge 3.38 extravgp=1.
> EXECUTE.
> VARIABLE LABEL extravgp 'extraversion group'.
> *Assigning value labels to the extraversion group response options.
> VALUE LABELS extravgp
> 0 'low extraversion (below median)'
> 1 'high extraversion (at or above median)'.

Note that newly created variables always appear to the right of the last column of your data file. If you want to see them, scroll all the way to the end of your file or for a shortcut just press control + forward arrow. (Pressing control + backward arrow will take you to the first column of your data file.)

Computing Variables: z-Scores

The use of standardized scores (z-scores, with a mean of 0 and a standard deviation of 1) is common enough in many statistical analyses that it is worth mentioning how you can easily obtain them. Selecting "Descriptive Statistics" and "Descriptives" on the Analyze menu, choose the variable you want to standardize, and check the box to request saving the standardized values as a variable. The new variable will be automatically saved with a z on the front of its name, and you can immediately see it added to the end of your data file. For example, these commands would produce the standardized scores for your age variable in a new variable called *zage*.

> *Obtaining standardized (z) scores for the age variable.
> DESCRIPTIVES age
> /SAVE.

One complication is that if you run this command more than once on the same data file, SPSS will create a new, identical copy of the standardized variable each time (with ambiguous default names such as *Zsco01, Zsco02*). If this happens, you can delete these extra variables and just keep the first one, which would have been properly named.

Computing Variables: Scales

To compute scales that combine several items, you should follow the instructions provided by the creator of the scale, whenever these are available. Most scales are computed using the mean or sum of a set of items or a count of specific ways of responding to those items. To paste the appropriate commands, you can click the "Compute Variable" command under the Transform menu. But computation commands are often easier to do by typing; the following are a few examples to illustrate the most common kinds of computations.

The following command computes a scale (called *newvariable*) that is the mean of four variables:

```
COMPUTE newvariable=MEAN(var1, var2, var3, var4).
EXECUTE.
```

The following similar command computes the scale to be the sum of four variables:

```
COMPUTE newvariable=SUM(var1, var2, var3, var4).
EXECUTE.
```

The following command computes the scale to be the count of how many times the participant's response was the option coded "8."

```
COUNT newvariable=var1 var2 var3 var4 (8).
EXECUTE.
```

Commands can be written to compute variables based on all kinds of mathematical, statistical, and miscellaneous functions. You can even create a variable for which the values are those from the previous row of another variable (using the LAG function). Many options are available in the "Compute Variables" dialogue window, on the Transform menu. The following are some examples to illustrate some of the most common computation commands that are useful for computing interaction terms, transforming variables to reduce skewness, and so on:

*The product of two variables.
    COMPUTE newvariable=var1*var2.
*A variable squared.
    COMPUTE newvariable=var1**2.
*A variable cubed.
    COMPUTE newvariable=var1**3.
*The square root of a variable.
    COMPUTE newvariable =SQRT(var1).
*The natural log of a variable.
    COMPUTE newvariable= ln(var1).
*A variable divided by 100.
    COMPUTE newvariable=var1/100.

To illustrate how you'd put computation commands together to create a scale, the following example shows all the steps used to compute the extraversion scale from the BFI. The scale is the mean of eight items, with the three low extraversion items (e.g., bfi21, "tends to be quiet") reversed so that all items are scored in the direction of high extraversion. Note that although an EXECUTE line is necessary for computations to run, you don't need to include this line after every individual computation, as long as there is an EXECUTE line at the very end of the set.

*Reversing extraversion items phrased backward on the Big Five Inventory (BFI).
COMPUTE bfi6r=6-bfi6.
COMPUTE bfi21r=6-bfi21.
COMPUTE bfi31r=6-bfi31.
EXECUTE.
VARIABLE LABEL bfi6r 'REV-is reserved'.
VARIABLE LABEL bfi21r 'REV-tends to be quiet'.
VARIABLE LABEL bfi31r 'REV-is sometimes shy, inhibited'.

*Computing extraversion scale from Big Five Inventory (BFI).
COMPUTE extraversion=mean(bfi1, bfi6r, bfi11, bfi16, bfi21r, bfi26, bfi31r, bfi36).
EXECUTE.
VARIABLE LABEL extraversion 'extraversion scale from BFI'.

Scale Reliability Analysis

Typically, when you are using a scale, you'll need to include in your paper information about its internal consistency reliability. I strongly recommend running the reliability analysis right away for every scale you create because it will allow you to identify any problems with your scale before you use it in other analyses. You can obtain the reliability commands by selecting "Scale" on the Analyze menu. A useful trick is to copy and paste the list of items from the COMPUTE command into the "VARIABLES" line of the RELIABILITY command, as follows:

> *Examining reliability of extraversion scale from the Big Five Inventory (BFI).
> RELIABILITY
> /VARIABLES=bfi1, bfi6r, bfi11, bfi16, bfi21r, bfi26, bfi31r, bfi36
> /SCALE('ALL VARIABLES') ALL
> /MODEL=ALPHA
> /SUMMARY=TOTAL.

This analysis will tell you how internally consistent the items in your scale are—in other words, how well the items tend to be answered similarly or "go together." You can see from the output in Figure 4.3 that the alpha coefficient (α) is .885. The analysis also produces a table you can use to verify that each item in the scale is positively correlated with the scale total. If any item is not positively correlated with the scale total, you should carefully check it for errors because often such a result indicates that you forgot to reverse score the item or set its missing data codes. In this example, the "Corrected Item–Total Correlation" column reassures you that all eight items are positively correlated with the total, as anticipated.

Reliability Statistics

Cronbach's Alpha	N of Items
.885	8

Item-Total Statistics

	Scale Mean if Item Deleted	Scale Variance if Item Deleted	Corrected Item–Total Correlation	Cronbach's Alpha if Item Deleted
bfi1 is talkative	23.1568	35.448	.766	.859
bfi6r REV-is reserved	24.0852	36.555	.677	.868
bfi11 is full of energy	22.9609	41.254	.460	.887
bfi16 generates a lot of enthusiasm	22.9663	39.094	.642	.873
bfi21r REV-tends to be quiet	23.8744	34.571	.790	.856
bfi26 has an assertive personality	23.6852	39.577	.434	.893
bfi31r REV-is sometimes shy, inhibited	24.2149	34.992	.723	.863
bfi36 is outgoing, sociable	22.9501	36.405	.764	.860

Figure 4.3

Reliability output. From IBM SPSS Statistics, Version 24.0, by IBM Corporation, 2016, Armonk, NY: IBM Corporation. Copyright 2016 by IBM Corporation.

Working With Subsets of Your Sample

It is relatively common to conduct analyses that involve only selected cases from your sample or separate portions of your sample. For example, if you want to do an analysis only on the women in your sample or you want to do the analysis separately for the women and the men, you should insert the applicable FILTER or SPLIT FILE command into your command file immediately before the analysis in question and insert a command to resume using the entire sample immediately after it. Do not be concerned if several analysis commands in a row repeat the same filter or split file specifications. Repeating these lines each time will allow your analyses to run properly even if they are run in a different order.

The following is an example of analyses that applied a filter command to only include women who reported being in relationships. You could obtain this filter command using the "Select Cases" option on the Data menu.

*Examining age and relationship duration of women in relationships.
*Including only women in relationships in the next analyses.

USE ALL.
COMPUTE filter_$=(single=0 & gender=1).
FILTER BY filter_$.
EXECUTE.
DESCRIPTIVES age yrsrel.
*Removing previously applied filter.
USE ALL.

The following is an example of analyses that used a split file command to examine men and women separately. You could obtain this command using the "Split File" option on the Data menu.

*Examining age and relationship duration separately by gender.
*The next analyses are run separately by gender.
SORT CASES BY gender.
SPLIT FILE SEPARATE BY gender.
DESCRIPTIVES age yrsrel.
*Removing previously applied file split.
SPLIT FILE OFF.

Data Analysis

Though only basic descriptive statistics were obtained in the previous examples, any type of analysis could be pasted into your command file the same way. Remember to add comments to your command file right before each analysis to help keep track of what each one is for. For projects involving multiple data analysis sessions, you should use a data analysis log (in your Logs folder; see Chapter 2) to keep a record of all the analyses you tried and all the decisions you made. Listing the names of the relevant command files in your data analysis log will also be helpful for when you have to relocate the commands you created for a specific analysis.

Analyses often proceed in a series of steps that build on one another. Therefore, as you get more comfortable with SPSS command language, you may find you can most easily create analysis commands by sequentially pasting and modifying them. Start by using the SPSS Analyze menu to paste the command for the first analysis in a series. For subsequent analyses, you will often be able to duplicate and edit the previous command, just changing a variable or a specification as needed. (If you do this, you will notice that pasting SPSS commands results in more lines than are necessary, and you can simplify your commands by deleting optional parts.)

When managing and analyzing your data, make sure to follow through with how you promised to do these things in your proposal, institutional review board submission, data management plan, and/or study preregistration. In fact, substantial changes to these plans would require first seeking new approval from the board, funding agency, journal, or professor who had approved the previous version. Nevertheless, expectations that researchers formally document their hypotheses and plans for handling their data ahead of time should not be misinterpreted as somehow prohibiting or discouraging them from doing extra analyses. It is also fine to include extra, more exploratory measures in your research proposals in addition to the specific hypotheses you are planning to test. Creative exploration is a large part of how theories and hypotheses are developed for testing in future studies, and science will not benefit from stifling it.

CONCLUDING COMMENTS

This chapter focused on creating command files to manage and analyze your data. These command files will also serve as documentation that could allow someone else to replicate these processes from scratch. In fact, the command files discussed in this chapter, together with the data files discussed in Chapter 3, are the key items you need to keep for your project. Some readers may be surprised to realize that this book has no chapter on output files (i.e., printouts of your results). Though you can keep some optional output files if you would like to, output files are not all that important because using your command files and your data files you can recreate your output any time in seconds. Besides, verifying your results means reproducing them, not just verifying that they were on your printout.

5

Your Replication Documentation

So far, you've read about the steps involved in managing and analyzing data and about how to save the project files, data, and commands recording your steps. In this chapter, I discuss how to prepare a *Replication Documentation* folder to accompany the paper you write about your research project. Although you can start preparing your Replication Documentation folder before your paper is finished, the information in the folder is meant to correspond to the information in your paper, so you should concentrate on finishing your paper first.

Putting together your Replication Documentation folder largely involves copying from the data files and command files you have already created for your project. However, the information in your Replication Documentation folder should be specific to your finished paper and may not necessarily address all the data you have or all the analyses you did. Moreover, because replication documentation is meant to be publicly

http://dx.doi.org/10.1037/0000068-005
Managing Your Research Data and Documentation, by K. R. Berenson

shared, it may be necessary to omit some information to protect participant confidentiality and adhere to copyright laws. In short, the Replication Documentation folder you create now often contains only a subset of the information you created for your private use.

Your Replication Documentation folder also differs from your private files in that it is specifically designed to be user-friendly for people outside your research team. Hence, the files in this folder are accompanied by additional instructions and basic information (i.e., the read-me and data appendix documents), as well as comments that directly refer to the page of your paper on which the relevant results are reported. The data files from the final analyses reported in your paper—with the data set already cleaned and the variables already computed—will also be provided for the convenience of individuals wanting to replicate your results.

PARTICIPANT CONFIDENTIALITY CONSIDERATIONS FOR REPLICATION DOCUMENTATION

The ethical responsibility of researchers to share their data for the sake of reproducibility presents unique challenges for researchers of human psychology. Compared with researchers studying animal behavior, proteins, or gross national products, researchers studying human psychology cannot always share their data quite so readily because the ethical principles guiding data sharing and confidentiality sometimes come into conflict with one another. Of course, not all psychology research involves confidential data, and you may not have to deal with confidentiality issues for your current research project. Nevertheless, all researchers should be aware of these issues as the sharing of data in public archives increasingly becomes the new norm.

Back when you were first designing your project, you weighed the risks and benefits of collecting the data you did from your participants. Now, as you prepare your Replication Documentation folder to make your data accessible to the public, you should take some time to reflect on these issues again and be alert to the possibility that some portions of your data set may be unethical to share—especially if you're doing research in a small community or if any aspects of your research are personal or sensitive.

Many human subject variables that would be completely acceptable (or even so benign as to seem trivial) if you were collecting and reporting them in terms of descriptive statistics and associations could pose serious ethical problems when it comes to sharing the actual data. For instance, it is one thing to report statistics that summarize a set of personal interviews or essays, but quite another thing to make copies of those actual interviews or essays available to the public. Likewise, it compromises no one's confidentiality to report in a paper that 4% of students at your college are majoring in particular subjects, 2% identify as belonging to particular groups, and 5% have a history of being in a specific upsetting situation that people are often reluctant to admit without anonymity. Reporting the associations (e.g., correlation coefficients) between these variables would also be safe from the standpoint of confidentiality. But it is an entirely different thing to publicly share the data set containing this information and allow people to see that the participant who is a double major in a rare combination of subjects and a member of rare groups reported having been in that specific upsetting situation. Access to your data set may allow someone with knowledge of your sample to recognize particular individuals and learn things those individuals never consented to broadcast when they volunteered to be anonymous participants in your research project. Even if you think the risk of someone recognizing your participants is low, it is still your duty to prevent such a violation of confidentiality from happening at all. The solution is to strip your data files of information that is particularly individualized in nature, such as open-ended responses (in the participant's words) and specific details about demographic characteristics.

Open-ended responses, such as essays, interview responses, or write-ins, often have to be omitted from the copies of the data you place in your Replication Documentation folder. Researchers sometimes ask participants to provide open-ended responses on personal topics, such as their personal values, how they feel about their parents, their first sexual experience, a time they failed at something, or their symptoms of anxiety. Because participants' words are unique enough to be potentially recognizable, you should not make open-ended responses publicly accessible in an archive or report, even anonymously, unless you obtained the participants' explicit consent to do so. Of course, psychology researchers usually convert open-ended, personal responses into numeric codes for data analysis. After members of your research team have coded each response (e.g., by counting the number of times the participant used the word *I*, rating the positivity of the emotions expressed from 1 to 10, or counting how many diagnostic criteria for generalized anxiety disorder the participant met, and so on), the resulting numeric codes would be completely impersonal and fine to include in your Replication Documentation data files. You share the codes in your replication documentation, but omit responses that are in participants' idiosyncratic words.

Variables indicating very specific demographic characteristics should often be omitted from publicly shared data files as well. Few individuals from any community were born on a particular day, so including participants' dates of birth in a data file could inadvertently reveal their identities. If your study was conducted in a small community in which particular demographic characteristics are underrepresented, including specific information about those characteristics in your data file could likewise violate the confidentiality of the community members known to be identified with them. Fortunately, as with open-ended responses, details about specific demographic characteristics and dates are almost never required for someone to replicate the results you report in your paper, and you can omit them from the data files you share without hesitation. Even if these details are somehow reported in your description of your sample, that fact alone is not sufficient reason to risk violating participants' confidentiality, and you can still omit them.

For example, if your study compares students involved in fraternities or sororities with those who are not members of these organizations, you're likely to specify in your paper how many participants were members of which organizations (e.g., "Three students belonged to this fraternity, one student belonged to this other fraternity, two belonged to this sorority"). Including this information in your paper is helpful for characterizing your sample and poses no ethical problem because it does not allow anyone to recognize the data provided by any one individual. An ethical problem only emerges if you share the actual data file and therefore allow people to see and potentially recognize the unique combinations of responses provided by individual participants.

Because most of your analyses in the results section of your paper would just be making comparisons on a more general variable called "member," indicating whether the student was a member of a fraternity or sorority (0 = *no*, 1 = *yes*), it is not necessary to share the variable with specific details about which participants are in which organizations. For the sake of reducing the risk of harm to your participants, at only a small cost to the openness of science, you would delete the detailed variable and just share the more general one. You should do the same thing for variables containing detailed information about any other potentially identifying characteristic (e.g., race or ethnicity, age, sexual orientation, gender identification, nation or state of origin, religious affiliation, majors and minors, club or team membership, dorm of residence). Of course, if these variables are included in your central analyses, you should make every effort to share them in your Replication Documentation files. But most of the time, relatively rare characteristics are grouped into a vague "other/none of the above" category anyway for the purposes of statistical analysis, and you can still omit more specific, potentially revealing details from your data sets.

COPYRIGHT CONSIDERATIONS FOR REPLICATION DOCUMENTATION

You must not include information in your Replication Documentation folder that you do not have the right to share publicly. Most research materials are available to use and share as long as you cite them—but some are not. For example, because IQ tests would be useless if everyone knew and practiced the questions in advance, ethical use of an IQ test involves a duty not to distribute it publicly. Many materials used for clinical, educational, and personality assessment have similar restrictions for reasons relating to ethics and/or intellectual property rights. If your research study uses restricted materials as part of its procedures, make sure not to reveal any of their content (e.g., the wording of items) in your variable labels, variable label commands, or explanatory comments or elsewhere in your Replication Documentation files.

THE CONTENTS OF YOUR REPLICATION DOCUMENTATION FOLDER

Read-Me, Paper, and Related Documents

The read-me document is meant to orient readers to your Replication Documentation folder and everything they would need to replicate your results. It includes a description or list of all the files inside the folder and step-by-step instructions on how to use to them to conduct a replication. Make sure to specify what statistical software will be needed to run the files. Save the final version of your read-me document as a PDF. You will also store in this folder a copy of the final version of your paper and a copy of any official documentation of the plans you made for your data analyses (e.g., formal preregistration).

Replication Data for Processing

The files in this folder begin as duplicates of the corresponding files you have created for your own use. For many projects, these data files will not need any modifications. However, there are circumstances in which the publicly shared data files must differ from private ones to protect participant confidentiality and comply with copyright laws, as discussed in the previous sections. Beyond this, if your paper is based on only a portion of a larger data set, it may make sense to share publicly only the relevant portions (rather than the entire, larger project). Keep in mind that before making decisions about what portions of a data set to publicly share, you must first obtain the approval and input of all the researchers with control over the data set.

The reason you don't usually have to include copies of your Original Data files in your Replication Documentation folder is that the shareable portions of these files are typically quite redundant with the files in your Replication Data for Processing folder. Of course, if researchers request to see the relevant portions of your Original Data files and/or the commands you used to convert them into your Data for Processing files, you would share with them everything you can, consistent with the American Psychological Association's (2017) *Ethical Principles of Psychologists and Code of Conduct.*

Replication Command Files

This folder contains the command file(s) one would need to reproduce the results reported in your paper, starting from your Replication Data for Processing file(s). Commands for computations and analyses are presented in the order your paper presented them (to the extent this is possible), and comments include the corresponding page number of your paper on which the results appear. For some projects, you may be able to include all your commands in a single command file. For other projects, it may make more sense to split up the commands into a series of separate files, with names that reflect their specific purpose.

To create these command files, duplicate the relevant command files you previously created for private use and save them into the Replication Command files (in your Replication Documentation folder). Then edit them as needed. Make sure the top of each command file specifies the correct data file (in your Replication Documentation folder) with which it should be used. To the extent you can, make sure all the commands needed for your paper are included and that commands for analyses are presented in the order in which they are reported in your paper. Omit any information from your command files that would be inconsistent with confidentiality or copyright concerns (e.g., details about an individual participant or the wording of a questionnaire item that is not publicly available).

Edit the comments preceding each analysis command so they refer to the page of your paper on which the results are presented. If your private command files contained any commands for extra analyses you didn't end up mentioning in your paper, you don't need to keep them in your Replication Command files (and if you decide you want to include them, your comments should indicate that the analysis was supplemental).

Because Replication Command files are intended for a stranger to be able to understand and use them, if further explanatory comments would be helpful to that hypothetical stranger, you should add them.

Check the completeness and accuracy of your Replication Command file(s) by trying to reproduce your results from scratch. If any commands won't run, look for punctuation or spelling errors and check the order in which commands are being processed. Fix mistakes and run your Replication Command file(s) again until everything works the way it should. You will then save the final data set(s) from these analyses in the Replication Analysis Data folder, as described in the upcoming section.

Save copies of the final versions of your Replication Command files as a PDF so they can be opened and read without an active SPSS license. These files will have the same names as your Replication Command files and contain the same information, except they will have a ".pdf" extension instead of ".sps."

Replication Analysis Data (With Data Appendix)

Replication Analysis Data files, in which your data are already labeled and cleaned and your variables already computed, are the data files used for the analyses reported in your paper. Of course, anyone should be able to recreate your Replication Analysis Data file(s) from scratch, using your Replication Data for Processing and your Replication Command files. Nevertheless, your Replication Analysis Data file(s) should be provided for anyone who wants to look at the data set you analyzed without having to go through all the effort to recreate it.

If you saved an Analysis Data file or a Working Data file for your private use when you first did your analyses, the Replication Analysis Data file you create now will turn out to be similar. But do not create your Replication Analysis Data file by duplicating a private file. Why not? Well, for one thing, your Replication Analysis Data files should have the same modifications for confidentiality and copyright as your Replication Data for Processing files. Moreover, you need to run a test of your replication documentation anyway—to show that you can reproduce your Analysis Data files and results by running your Replication Command files on your Replication Data for Processing. You'll create your Replication Analysis Data file by doing this test (as mentioned in the previous section).

A Data Appendix provides information about every variable in your Replication Analysis Data file(s). You'll create the appendix by running the "Codebook" command (found under "Reports" on the Analyze menu in SPSS). Run this command for all the variables in the order they appear in the Replication Analysis Data file. For each variable, the output will display the variable name, variable label, and any value labels, as well as information about the type and format of the variable. A count of the valid and missing cases will be provided. For categorical variables, the output will include a frequency table. For quantitative variables, the output will include the mean, standard deviation, and quartiles (remember the 50th percentile is also the median). Of course, to create a good Data Appendix, you have to have assigned useful variable labels and value labels to the entire data set.

Convert the output of your Codebook analysis to a PDF file called Data Appendix (by right clicking to export the output as a PDF, or by clicking "Print" and choosing the print to PDF option). Keep this document with the data set it corresponds to, inside your Replication Analysis Data folder. If you have more than one Replication Analysis Data file, give your files and their associated appendixes names that distinguish them. For example, you might have a tall data file (see Appendix C) called "Replication Analysis Data—Response Time by Trial," as well as a data file called "Replication Analysis Data—Extraversion Study," and each of these would have its own data appendix document.

Because your replication documentation would allow any reader to reproduce your results easily, it is not necessary to archive the output files from the analyses you conducted. Nevertheless, people sometimes like to save PDF copies of their output files, for the sake of convenience. If you save the output from your analyses, you would keep it organized in the Replication Analysis Data folder.

Replication Source Data and Metadata (if Applicable)

If your project used data not collected by you and your project collaborators, but obtained from another source, you would include a copy of your Source Data folder and its Metadata subfolder in your Replication Documentation folder (unless the original source restricts sharing their data and materials). More information about source data and metadata is provided in Appendix A.

CONCLUDING COMMENTS

When complete, your Replication Documentation folder will contain everything a researcher reading your paper would need to replicate your results independently. You can see that it would be insufficient to provide only your output or analysis data because you would be keeping your reader in the dark about far too many of the decisions you made with your data. Replication requires documentation of all the data management and analysis steps you took from the beginning. And documenting those steps doesn't just mean jotting them down or even just talking about them in your paper. The replicability of research requires showing, not just telling.

Naturally, creating comprehensive and user-friendly documentation takes dedicated time and attention. Though your use of command files will get much easier and faster with practice, a Replication Documentation folder is not the sort of thing anyone should expect to quickly throw together in the last hour before a paper is due. But just as you would not submit your paper without a reference list, you should not consider replication documentation to be optional or supplemental. Documenting data management and analysis is a skill worth developing because none of the groundbreaking original research of the future is going to be done without it.

Appendix A
Source Data and Metadata

If you're obtaining your data set from another source, you'll need to keep a Source Data folder containing an untouched copy of the data set in whatever format you originally received it, along with a Metadata subfolder of information about the sources of the data set. These files are, in a sense, your "original data," but the term "source data" helps distinguish them from data that you've collected yourself. You'll also include a duplicate copy of your Source Data folder in your Replication Documentation folder, assuming the original source doesn't restrict re-sharing its contents.

The following instructions for documenting Source Data and Metadata folders are adapted from the Project TIER Protocol (Project TIER, 2016, pp. 8–9).

When user's guides and codebooks have been provided by the source, they should be stored in a "Supplements" subfolder within the Metadata folder. The Metadata folder should always contain a document called the Metadata Guide (which you'll save in PDF format when you're finished creating it). This document will systematically describe each of your Source Data files with the following information:

- An APA Style bibliographic citation for the data file.
- The date on which you downloaded or otherwise obtained the data file.
- Any unique identifiers (e.g., a digital object identifier, or DOI) for the data file.

⌁ Source Data and Metadata
    ⌁ U.S. Epidemiological Survey.xlsx
    ⌁ Canada Epidemiological Survey.xlsx
    ⌁ Metadata
        ⌁ Metadata Guide.pdf
        ⌁ Supplements
            ⌁ Codebook for U.S. Epidemiological Survey.pdf
            ⌁ Codebook for Canada Epidemiological Survey.pdf

Figure A.1

Source Data and Metadata folders.

- A description of how one can obtain the data file from the original source—for example, providing the URL and instructions for downloading it.
- All the information needed to use the data, such as identifying the available codebooks and user's guides (providing a citation for the source of these materials and a description of what information is contained in them). If any additional information is necessary to understand the structure and contents of the data file, this information should also be provided here.

To illustrate what this would look like, imagine that a student named Jane Doe completed a capstone project for the Psych 399 course at her college. In her project, she analyzed data she had downloaded from the websites of government agencies conducting epidemiological surveys in the United States and Canada. Jane would, therefore, include the Source Data and Metadata subfolders depicted in Figure A.1 in both her private Data Files folder and the shareable Replication Documentation folder she named "Replication Documentation for Doe PSY399."

a regular (one-row-per-case) data file. For example, one way of working with a tall data file from a multiple-trial experiment or a diary is to get some summary statistic (e.g., the mean, median, or standard deviation) for each participant and merge that variable into a data file containing other participant information. The following example uses means obtained in SPSS, but the procedures would be basically the same for any statistic obtained for each participant, in any statistical program.

Using the tall data file shown in the earlier example, we could run an analysis to get the mean RT for each participant. To paste the commands to do this, click on "Means" (found under "Compare Means" on the Analyze menu). Put the ID variable in the independents list and the RT variable in the dependents list. Keep the output simple by adjusting the options to ask for just the means (not other things such as the SD and n). The pasted command would be as follows:

*Obtaining the mean RT for each participant.
MEANS TABLES=RT BY ID
/CELLS=MEAN.

The output obtained from running this command appears in Figure B.3. To convert the table of means in the output into a data file, click on it and select "Export." Export the table as an Excel file, specifying the name of your new file (mean rt.xls) and the folder in which you want it saved. Next, find this file and open it in Excel (see Figure B.4). Delete the two heading rows ("Report" and "Mean") at the top and the "Total" row at the bottom (by highlighting/selecting the whole rows, right clicking, and selecting "Delete"). Re-save the Excel file with those three "junk" rows deleted.

Finally, open the Excel file with SPSS, and rename the RT variable to meanRT (a more accurate name) using the command RENAME VARIABLES (RT=meanRT), as described in Chapter 4 and shown in Figure B.5. Your file is now ready to merge with other standard data files containing information on your study participants, using the commands for merging files as described in Appendix F.

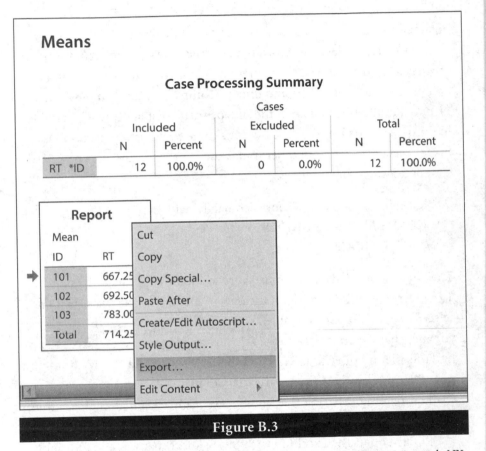

Figure B.3

Output file. From IBM SPSS Statistics, Version 24.0, by IBM Corporation, 2016, Armonk, NY: IBM Corporation. Copyright 2016 by IBM Corporation.

◢	A	B	C	D
1	**Report**			
2	Mean			
3	ID	RT		
4	101	667.25		
5	102	692.50		
6	103	783.00		
7	Total	714.25		
8				

Figure B.4

Output in Excel. From IBM SPSS Statistics, Version 24.0, by IBM Corporation, 2016, Armonk, NY: IBM Corporation. Copyright 2016 by IBM Corporation.

	ID	meanRT	var
1	101	667.25	
2	102	692.50	
3	103	783.00	
4			

Figure B.5

Mean RT. From IBM SPSS Statistics, Version 24.0, by IBM Corporation, 2016, Armonk, NY: IBM Corporation. Copyright 2016 by IBM Corporation.

Appendix C
Data Entry

The following is the procedure for using double entry to create a data file free of careless errors. Create an Excel spreadsheet with variable names on the top of each column and the ID variable on the far left, with one row per case. If you need to enter a lot of variables, split them up so that each file contains no more than 200 or so. After you have created the blank spreadsheet, make another copy of it, and label the two files Entry 1 and Entry 2. For example, if your project involved personality questionnaires and family history questionnaires that were administered on paper, you would put a Data Entry folder inside your Original Data folder. Inside the Data Entry folder, you would have spreadsheets called "Personality Questionnaire Entry 1" and "Personality Questionnaire Entry 2," as well as "Family History Entry 1" and "Family History Entry 2." Decide on (at least) two individuals who will carefully enter the data into Entry 1 and Entry 2 for each questionnaire. You may want to keep data entry logs (lists of which ID numbers have been entered), especially for a large or complex data set.

Decide in advance how individuals entering data ought to handle situations in which participants mark more than one answer or make a mark between two answers. Also decide on a "missing data" code for items participants skipped. For this, choose a number that is not a valid answer anywhere in the data to be entered, so that it's always easy to distinguish between missing and valid answers (a number such as 99 or 999 is usually chosen). Hand-written answers should be typed exactly as they appear. The point is to decide on enough rules so that two individuals doing careful data entry will end up typing the same information independently.

After all the data have been entered twice, find and correct any data entry errors by comparing the two data files. This process is called *data reconciliation*. In Excel, open both Entry 1 and Entry 2 of the file you want to reconcile and sort the cases in each file (one at a time). To sort each file, select/highlight all the data by clicking the upper left corner of the spreadsheet, and then select "Sort Cases by ID Number" on the Data menu. Make sure both versions of the spreadsheet contain the same ID numbers.

Now, open a new Excel document, type "Entry 1" in the first line, and paste all the data from the Entry 1 file in the rows below. Skip a few rows, type "Entry 2" in a line, and paste the Entry 2 data below this. Click "Find" and "Replace" on the Edit menu, replacing all "NULL" answers with 99 or 999 (to make your file easier to look at). Skip a few rows beneath the last filled line of your Excel file, and type "Reconciled Data." Paste the variable names from either the Entry 1 or Entry 2 document on the row beneath this and the ID numbers in the same column as in the other files. The layout of the "Reconciled data" section should be identical to that of Entry 1 and Entry 2, but it should contain no data. The example in Figure C.1 shows a data set with three participants' data.

To identify the discrepancies between Entry 1 and Entry 2, you'll need to type a logical test into the first empty square of the Reconciled data section by selecting the relevant square and clicking the "Insert Function" button. Select "Logical," then "IF," and enter the appropriate information in the dialog box that appears.

In this example, B3=B10 was typed into the Logical_test box, 0 was typed in the Value_if_true box, and 777 was typed in the Value_if_false box. This tells Excel that first empty square (Cell B17) should show whether Cell B3 is identical to Cell B10. If true, Cell B17 should return a 0; if false, Cell B17 should return 777. The value 777 means nothing and was only chosen to stand out relatively easily in a field of zeros. The key will be for you to determine which cell should correspond to which cell in

B17		▼	f_x	=IF(B3=B10,0,777)	
	A	B	C	D	E	F
1	Entry 1					
2	ID	bfi1	bfi2	bfi3	bfi4	bfi5
3	101	3	4	2	999	3
4	102	4	4	3	4	1
5	103	3	5	3	3	2
6						
7						
8	Entry 2					
9	ID	bfi1	bfi2	bfi3	bfi4	bfi5
10	101	3	4	2	999	3
11	102	4	3	3	4	1
12	103	3	5	3	3	2
13						
14						
15	Reconciled data					
16	ID	bfi1	bfi2	bfi3	bfi4	bfi5
17	101	0	0	0	0	0
18	102	0	777	0	0	0
19	103	0	0	0	0	0

Figure C.1

Data reconciliation. From IBM SPSS Statistics, Version 24.0, by IBM Corporation, 2016, Armonk, NY: IBM Corporation. Copyright 2016 by IBM Corporation.

your Excel spreadsheet, analogous to the way B17 reflects the outcome of a comparison between B3 and B10 in this one.

After you've added information, click "OK." Then drag the lower right corner of that first cell until the function is applied to all cells in the Reconciled data section, as illustrated in Figure C.1. Each 777 indicates a discrepancy between the information in Entry 1 and Entry 2 for that particular item. In this example, we see a discrepancy for Item bfi2 in Participant 102, where Entry 1 says 4 and Entry 2 says 3. Systematically resolve each discrepancy by looking through the paper files to figure out what the correct response should be. Make the necessary corrections to the relevant cells in both the Entry 1 and Entry 2 sections of your current Excel document (until they are identical). This will cause the 777s in the Reconciled data section to change to 0s. When there are no 777s left in the Reconciled data section, copy and paste either the Entry 1 or Entry 2 section (they should be identical) into an Excel sheet on its own, and save it in your Original Data folder.

Appendix D
Labeling and Renaming
Many Variables Efficiently

If you have a lot of variables to label (e.g., a long questionnaire), you can speed this process up by using the Table function in Word. Insert a table with five columns and one row per variable into a Word document. Column 1 should contain the words VARIABLE LABEL (as shown in Table D.1). You can type it once and copy and paste it into as many rows as you need. Column 2 should contain your list of variable names. Column 3 should contain a single quotation mark. Column 4 should contain your variable labels, which you can often easily copy and paste from an existing document such as a copy of the questionnaire. Column 5 should contain a quotation mark and a period. After you have finished creating this table, select the whole thing and under "Table," select "Convert" and "Convert Table to Text." Put a single space in the box for a custom separator (put your cursor in the box and press the space bar once). Your table will be converted into the correct set of commands, which you can then paste into your SPSS syntax window. You can use a similar procedure to rename many variables at once, as in Table D.2.

Table D.1
Variable Label Table

VARIABLE LABEL	bfi1	'	is talkative	.
VARIABLE LABEL	bfi2	'	tends to find fault in others	.
VARIABLE LABEL	bfi3	'	does a thorough job	.
VARIABLE LABEL	bfi4	'	is depressed, blue	.
VARIABLE LABEL	bfi5	'	is original, comes up with new ideas	.

Table D.2
Rename Variables Table

RENAME VARIABLES (	Whatwasthehighestgradeyoufinished	=	edlevel	).
RENAME VARIABLES (	V1	=	income	).
RENAME VARIABLES (	V2	=	kids	).
RENAME VARIABLES (	V3	=	employed	).

Appendix E
Importing Data Files

Text (.txt) or comma-separated (.csv) files can be imported into SPSS using the "Read Text Data" command under the File menu: Just paste the import commands into a command file that you can save and run. If all your variables are numeric, importing will be straightforward. Small complications can sometimes arise when importing string variables (open-ended responses that include nonnumeric characters), but you can solve these easily if you know what to look for.

Check the preview window to see whether all the columns line up as they should in your data set. If it doesn't look right, by unchecking that box make sure SPSS isn't automatically separating the columns whenever there is a space in the data. Another common source of confusion occurs when someone types a comma into their open-ended response, and SPSS incorrectly interprets the comma as the separation between two variables. You can fix this by first opening the data file into an Excel spreadsheet and using the "Replace" feature to eliminate all the commas (replacing them with nothing, a blank space, or a different punctuation mark).

When importing string variables, each of them will automatically be assigned the column width (number of characters) associated with the longest response, resulting in variables that have a wide variety of peculiar widths. If you are going to merge these files, they will have to have consistent widths, so you should change all the string column widths to a large, round number by editing your import commands slightly. In the following example, you can see the import commands a student named James Bond might paste for importing a file called "September questionnaires.csv." The import command "ID F8.0" is setting the ID variable to be a numeric variable with up to eight characters and no decimal places. The command "mood F8.2" is setting the mood rating variable to be a numeric variable with up to eight characters and two decimal places. The command "thoughts A231" is automatically setting the string variable called "thoughts," (in which participants were asked to type whatever thoughts crossed their mind) to have 231 characters because, apparently, the longest response given by any of the participants must have contained 231 characters. To change this variable to have a large, round number of characters (500 characters), you would edit the pasted command to say "thoughts A500" instead of "thoughts A231."

*Commands for importing the September Questionnaires data set into SPSS.
*The csv version of the data set is called September Questionnaires in the Original Data folder.
GET DATA/TYPE=TXT
/FILE=E:\Bond, J PSY399\Data files\Original Data\September questionnaires.csv'
/DELCASE=LINE
/DELIMITERS=","
/QUALIFIER="''
/ARRANGEMENT=DELIMITED
/FIRSTCASE=2
/IMPORTCASE=ALL
/VARIABLES=
ID F8.0
mood F8.2
thoughts A231.
*Saving the SPSS version as September Questionnaires in the Data for Processing folder.
SAVE OUTFILE=
'E:\Bond, J PSY399\Data files\Data for Processing\September questionnaires.sav'
/COMPRESSED.

Appendix F
Merging Data Files

To merge data files, use the SPSS merge commands found under the Data menu by pasting them into your command file and running them. There are two ways to merge files ("Add Cases" and "Add Variables" under the "Merge Files" feature), and you'll have to decide which type of merge you are trying to do. Adding cases involves two data sets with the same variables and different cases; adding variables involves two data sets with different variables and the same cases.

When adding cases, it is essential that all the variables you wish to keep in the merged data set have the same names and variable properties (e.g., being numeric vs. string, and the column width). If the Add Cases dialog box lists any of these variables in the "Unpaired Variables" section, you'll want to fix their variable properties to be identical across the two data sets before proceeding with the merge command.

When adding variables, you must first sort both files by the ID variable using the sort command under the Data menu. When the Add Variables dialog box appears (as shown in Figure F.1), put ID in the "Key Variables" section, and be sure that both "Match cases on key variables" and "Cases are sorted in order of key variables in both datasets" are checked. If any variables remain in the "Excluded Variables" section, it will be because a variable by the same name is found in both data sets, and you can fix that by renaming one of them if necessary. If you find yourself tempted

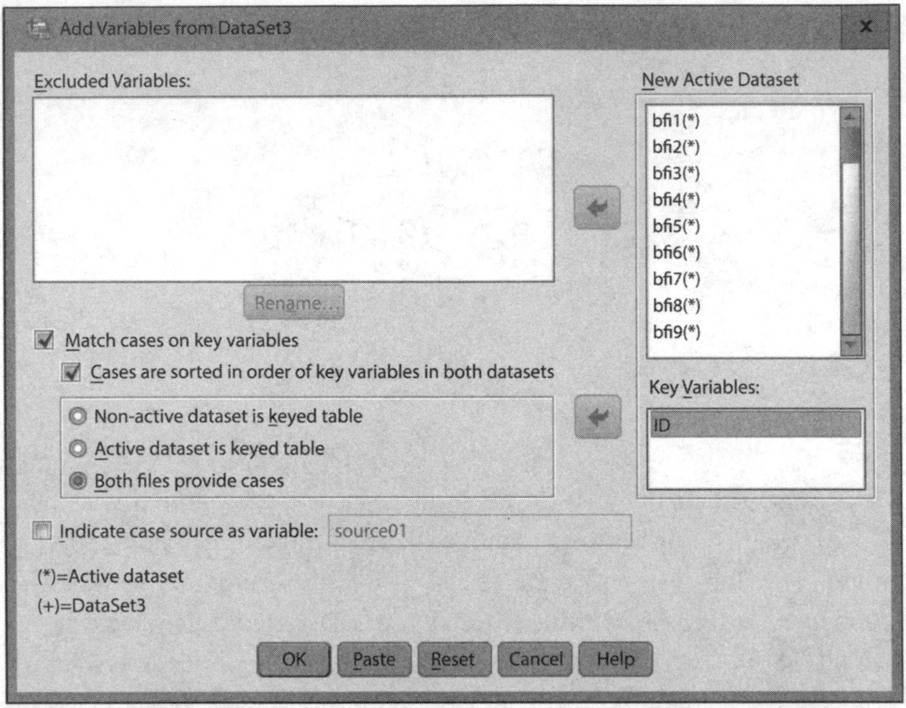

Figure F.1

Merge. From IBM SPSS Statistics, Version 24.0, by IBM Corporation, 2016, Armonk, NY: IBM Corporation. Copyright 2016 by IBM Corporation.

to copy and paste data instead of using merge commands, remember the dirty surgeon from the introduction chapter of this book. Accidentally pasting data into the wrong boxes could make your entire data set useless, and it can happen all too easily.

Appendix G
Estimating Missing Values

A comprehensive consideration of the procedures available for estimating missing values would be far beyond the scope of this book, particularly because it would require advanced statistical knowledge and specialized computer programs. Nevertheless, if your project is missing some data and you've decided it would be more appropriate to estimate some missing values than to exclude slightly incomplete or imperfect cases (as discussed in Chapter 4), this appendix can give you some guidelines about what you can do.

If you're missing data on a single, stand-alone item for a specific participant and have no other basis for estimating what the missing answer would have been, your best guess would typically be the mean score for your sample. To illustrate, if you're missing data about a participant's age and have no other information to help you estimate their age (e.g., their year of birth, how many years they've been in college), you could estimate that they are 19.73 years old, the mean age for the rest of the participants whose ages you know. As another example, perhaps you are missing data for a question asking whether the participant is Latino/Latina, with answer choices 0 = no, 1 = yes. In the absence of other information, your best estimate of the participant's missing answer to this question would be the sample mean, which in this case is 0.148, meaning that 14.8% of your sample is Latino/Latina. When the sample mean is not a meaningful value (e.g., for a nominal variable with multiple categories, such as race or ethnicity), your best estimate would be the most common value (the mode) for your sample instead. So if the largest racial or ethnic category in your sample is White/Caucasian, that would be your best guess for a participant whose race or ethnicity is unknown.

When data are missing from an item that is part of a set, you would not use the sample mean or mode as your estimate because the other items from the set can help you make a much better estimate. Consider an example in which one of the eight extraversion items from the Big Five Inventory (John, Donahue, & Kentle, 1991) seems to have been accidentally skipped by a participant. In this case, we do not know what the participant's answer ought to have been for Item bfi1, "is talkative," but we do have the participant's answers to seven other related items. Looking at how the extraversion items are worded, the missing item seems to be relatively similar in meaning to item bfi36 "is outgoing, sociable," and indeed, the correlation between bfi1 and bfi36 is .68. The fairly strong, significant association between the two items doesn't necessarily mean the participant would have given both items the same rating, though, because some items have higher average ratings than others. For example in this data set, participants seem somewhat more inclined to describe themselves as "outgoing/sociable" than to describe themselves as "talkative." The best way to estimate a missing value is to use statistical tools to systematically predict it from one or more items that are not missing. In this example you can try to predict what rating a participant would give for "is talkative" given what you know about how they rated "is outgoing, sociable."

You can make this prediction using linear regression. The following commands can be pasted using the Analyze menu to select "Regression" and "Linear."

```
*Conducting regression to obtain predicted values of bfi1 from bfi36.
REGRESSION
/DEPENDENT bfi1
/METHOD=ENTER bfi36.
```

The output from this analysis is shown in Figure G.1.

Coefficients[a]

Model		Unstandardized Coefficients		Standardized Coefficients		
		B	Std. Error	Beta	t	Sig.
1	(Constant)	.812	.238		3.408	.001
	bfi36 is outgoing, sociable	.738	.059	.680	12.529	.000

Figure G.1

Regression output. [a]Dependent Variable: bfi1 is talkative. From IBM SPSS Statistics, Version 24.0, by IBM Corporation, 2016, Armonk, NY: IBM Corporation. Copyright 2016 by IBM Corporation.

The predicted value from a simple regression equation with one predictor (x) uses the formula $b*x + c$, where b is the unstandardized coefficient for the slope, c is the constant, and $*$ is the symbol for multiplication. The output of your analysis indicates that the value of b is 0.738, and the constant is 0.812. You can therefore compute the predicted value of bfi1, which you will call "bfi1_pred," as follows:

*Computing predicted value of bfi1 from bfi36, using results from regression output.
COMPUTE bfi1_pred=.738*bfi36+.812.
EXECUTE.
VARIABLE LABEL bfi1_pred 'Predicted value of bfi1 based on value of bfi36'.
*Checking that mean of bfi1_pred is very, very close to mean of bfi1.
DESCRIPTIVES bfi1_pred bfi1.

It is a good idea to run descriptive statistics for the new variable bfi1_pred to make sure its mean is approximately equal to the mean of bfi1, as shown in the command language. In this example, the mean of bfi1_pred is 3.6842, and the mean of bfi1 is 3.6800, so they are quite close, as they should be. If you were to run an analysis examining the correlation between bfi1_pred and bfi1, it should be approximately equal to the correlation between bfi1 and bfi36. These analyses are supplemental in that they will not go into your paper, but they are still good to do, to check that you did not make major errors in reading your regression output or in typing the computation commands.

Of course, you would only use bfi1_pred instead of bfi1 for participants whose responses to bfi1 were missing in the first place. In other words, you have to recode missing values of bfi1 to be estimated by the regression equation obtained from your analysis, but use participants' actual responses to bfi1 when they exist. The estimated values usually have decimal places, whereas the actual values are usually round numbers, but don't be bothered by this discrepancy; the estimated values only have decimal places to be as accurately predicted as possible.

The following are two ways you can write commands to replace the missing values in bfi1 with the predicted values. The first way is to specify the ID numbers of the particular cases for which the value of bfi1 ought to be replaced with bfi1_pred. In this example, you'd only be replacing the (missing) value in bfi1 with bfi1_pred for the participant with ID #524.

*Replacing missing values of bfi1 with value predicted from regression output.
IF ID=524 bfi1=bfi1_pred.
EXECUTE.

Next is an alternative way to replace all the missing values in bfi1 with bfi1_pred without having to specify which particular cases have missing values. The complication is that assuming you have already told SPSS what values to ignore (because they are missing), you will have to temporarily undo that instruction for SPSS to recognize that these values need replacing. In the following command language, you are first reidentifying the missing values in bfi1 with 99s and then replacing all the 99s in bfi1 with bfi1_pred.

*Replacing missing values of bfi1 with value predicted from regression output.
RECODE bfi1 (SYSMIS=99).
IF bfi1=99 bfi1=bfi1_pred.
EXECUTE.

Advanced techniques for estimating missing values essentially build on the idea that you can statistically predict them from the values you have, but these techniques include more information from more variables to make a more accurate prediction. For example, multiple imputation is a method for handling missing data you may learn if you pursue graduate-level statistics courses. But until you have the expertise to consider other options, you can rely on the approaches described in this appendix to make the best estimates you can for replacing missing values.

References

American Psychological Association. (2010). *Publication manual of the American Psychological Association* (6th ed.). Washington, DC: Author.

American Psychological Association. (2017). *Ethical principles of psychologists and code of conduct* (2002, Amended June 1, 2010, and January 1, 2017). Retrieved from http://www.apa.org/ethics/code/index.aspx

Ball, R., & Medeiros, N. (2012). Teaching integrity in empirical research: A protocol for documenting data management and analysis. *The Journal of Economic Education, 43*, 182–189. http://dx.doi.org/10.1080/00220485.2012.659647

Blumenstyk, G. (2016, June 9). Liberal arts majors have plenty of job prospects, if they have some specific skills, too. *The Chronicle of Higher Education*. Retrieved from http://www.chronicle.com/article/Liberal-Arts-Majors-Have/236749/

Gilbert, D. T., King, G., Pettigrew, S., & Wilson, T. D. (2016). Comment on "Estimating the reproducibility of psychological science." *Science, 351*, 1037. http://dx.doi.org/10.1126/science.aad7243

IBM SPSS Statistics (Version 24.0) [Computer software]. Armonk, NY: IBM Corporation.

John, O. P., Donahue, E. M., & Kentle, R. L. (1991). *The Big Five Inventory—Versions 4a and 54*. Berkeley: University of California, Berkeley, Institute of Personality and Social Research.

Nosek, B. A., Alter, G., Banks, G. C., Borsboom, D., Bowman, S. D., Breckler, S. J., . . . Yarkoni, T. (2015). Promoting an open research culture. *Science, 348*, 1422–1425. http://dx.doi.org/10.1126/science.aab2374

Open Science Collaboration. (2015). Estimating the reproducibility of psychological science. *Science, 349*, aac4716. http://dx.doi.org/10.1126/science.aac4716

Owens, T. (2014). *Teaching integrity in empirical research: An interview with Richard Ball and Norm Medeiros.* Retrieved from https://blogs.loc.gov/thesignal/2014/09/teaching-integrity-in-empirical-research-an-interview-with-richard-ball-and-norm-medeiros/

Project TIER. (2016). *TIER protocol* (Version 3.0). Retrieved from http://www.projecttier.org/tier-protocol/

Simmons, J. P., Nelson, L. D., & Simonsohn, U. (2011). False-positive psychology. *Psychological Science, 22,* 1359–1366. http://dx.doi.org/10.1177/0956797611417632

Index

Academic psychology, culture of, 6
American Psychological Association
    (APA), 5, 71
Analysis Data, Replication, 13, 72–73
Analysis Data folder, 12, 26–27
APA (American Psychological
    Association), 5, 71
Approvals for study, 17

Ball, Richard, 7

Categorical variables, naming, 30
Command files
    adding commands to, 37
    additional instructions for running
        commands, 39
    assigning value labels, 45
    assigning variable labels, 43–45
    comments in, 40–41, 71–72
    creating/managing Data for
        Processing files, 42–43
    data analysis, 63–64
    easy access to, 41–42
    example of using, 37–39
    excluding cases, 51–54
    frequencies analyses, 46–47
    handling missing data, 48–51
    periods at end of commands, 39

    problems with, 39–40
    recoding items, 54–58
    renaming variables, 43
    Replication, 13, 71–72
    as research documentation, 35–36
    scale reliability analysis, 61–62
    scales, 59–61
    using missing data codes, 47–48
    value of, 33–36
    working with sample subsets,
        62–63
    z-scores, 58–59
Command Files folder, 8, 12–13,
    33–64
    and command files as
        documentation, 35–36
    number of files in, 36
    SPSS command files, 37–64. *See
        also* Command files
Comments, in command files, 40–41,
    71–72
Computing variables
    recoding items, 54–58
    scales, 59–61
    z-scores, 58–59
Confidentiality, 66–69
Consent forms, 21
Contact information file, 12, 21

About the Author

Kathy R. Berenson, PhD, is an assistant professor of psychology at Gettysburg College and a clinical psychologist who conducts research focused on cognitive/affective and interpersonal factors in psychological difficulties. She has many years of experience managing data for large, grant-funded studies and mentoring undergraduate research in the fields of personality and psychopathology.

About the Series Editor

Arthur M. Nezu, PhD, DHL, ABPP, is Distinguished University Professor of Psychology, professor of medicine, and professor of public health at Drexel University. In addition to currently serving as an associate editor of the *American Psychologist,* he has held several previous editorial positions, including editor of the *Journal of Consulting and Clinical Psychology*, associate editor of *Archives of Scientific Psychology*, editor of *The Behavior Therapist*, and chair of the Council of Editors for the American Psychological Association. His research and program development in clinical psychology and behavioral medicine have been supported by the National Cancer Institute, the National Institute of Mental Health, the Department of Veterans Affairs, the Department of Defense, the U.S. Air Force, and the Pew Fund. Dr. Nezu has also served on numerous research review panels for the National Institutes of Health and was previous president of both the Association of Behavioral and Cognitive Therapies and the American Board of Behavioral and Cognitive Psychology.